U.S.-China Economic and Security
Review Commission Staff Research Report
April 5, 2012

Indigenous Weapons Development in China's Military Modernization

Primary Author:
Amy Chang, USCC Research Fellow
for Military & National Security Affairs

Editor and Contributing Author:
John Dotson, USCC Research Coordinator

Cover Photos:

Top left: A view of the undercarriage of a PLA Air Force J-20 fighter during its maiden test flight, Jan. 11, 2011. Source: "CAC J-20," *Jane's All the World's Aircraft*, entry dated Jan. 28, 2011.

Bottom right: A *Yuan*-class submarine moored pierside. Source: Jeffrey Lewis, "Yuan Class Submarine," *ArmsControlWonk.com*, entry dated June 10, 2005.
http://lewis.armscontrolwonk.com/archive/639/yuan-class-submarine

Table of Contents

Glossary of Acronyms

A2/AD	Anti-Access/Area Denial
ABM	Anti-Ballistic Missile
AIP	Air Independent Propulsion
ASAT	Anti-Satellite
ASBM	Anti-Ship Ballistic Missile
C4ISR	Command, Control, Communications, Computer, Intelligence, Surveillance, and Reconnaissance
CCP	Chinese Communist Party
CSS-5	NATO designator for DF-21 medium range ballistic missile
DF-21D	Dongfeng-21D
DIA	U.S. Defense Intelligence Agency
DoD	U.S. Department of Defense
FY-1C	Variant of China's Fengyun-1 Series Sun-synchronous Orbit Weather Satellite
IOC	Initial Operational Capability
INF	Intermediate-Range Nuclear Forces Treaty
J-20	Jian-20 Fighter Aircraft (also known as XXJ and J-XX)
LTG	Lieutenant General
MaRV	Maneuverable Reentry Vehicle
MFA	Ministry of Foreign Affairs of the People's Republic of China
MRBM	Medium-range Ballistic Missile
NATO	North American Treaty Organization
ONI	Office of Naval Intelligence
PLA	People's Liberation Army
PLAN	People's Liberation Army Navy
PRC	People's Republic of China
R&D	Research and Development
S&T	Science and Technology
SS	Attack Submarine

Executive Summary

The rapid economic growth of the People's Republic of China (PRC) since 1979 has enabled the country to implement an extensive military modernization program. Since the mid-1990s, China's military reforms have accelerated and defense spending has steadily increased. In China's 2008 white paper on defense, China projected that it would lay a "solid foundation" for the development of national defense and the armed forces by 2010, "accomplish major mechanization and make major progress in informatization* by 2020," and reach modernization of its national defense and armed forces by the middle of the century.[1]

China's process of modernizing its armed forces has involved the development of indigenously designed weapons systems—some of which appeared to undergo a process of development, procurement, and/or deployment that outpaced the estimates of U.S. and other foreign observers. This paper specifically focuses on four key weapons platforms that have been discussed as "surprise" developments to U.S. analysts**:

- Type 039A/B/041 (Yuan-class) diesel-electric attack submarine
- SC-19 anti-satellite (ASAT) system
- Dongfeng-21D (DF-21D/CSS-5) anti-ship ballistic missile (ASBM)
- Jian-20 (J-20) stealth fighter aircraft[2]

Key Findings

Based on the four case studies covered in this report, there are no universal trends in publicly reported U.S. government analysis on the development of indigenous Chinese weapon systems. Evidence broadly suggests that U.S. analysts did not expect the emergence of the PLA Navy's *Yuan*-class submarine when the class was unveiled in 2004, much less that this class could potentially be utilizing air-independent propulsion (AIP) systems. On the other hand, U.S. officials were keenly aware of Chinese anti-satellite (ASAT) weapons development, and reports show that U.S. officials were also aware of potential ASAT testing activity in 2007,[3] although it is possible that the exact timing of the test was unexpected. However, while U.S. government analysts accurately anticipated several developments, such as the emergence of China's SC-19 ASAT system, China's selective transparency—or strategic deception that asserted opposition to the development of space weapons—may have misled foreign observers outside of military and intelligence channels.

There have been, however, identifiable cases of miscalculation regarding U.S. assessments on the development speed of Chinese indigenous weapons systems. While U.S. intelligence sources

---

* Informatization is the integration of information technology and communications networks into military strategy and weapons systems. For more on the topic, see Office of the Secretary of Defense, *Annual Report to Congress: Military and Security Developments Involving the People's Republic of China 2010* (Washington, DC: U.S. Department of Defense, 2010), p. 3.

** As used in this report, the term "U.S. analysts" refers to the broader China-watching community, including academics, journalists, and U.S. government analysts. Unless specifically noted, it does not refer solely to U.S. government analysts.

[1] Information Office of the State Council of the People's Republic of China, *China's National Defense in 2008*. http://www.china.org.cn/government/whitepaper/node_7060059.htm.

[2] The name "Chengdu Jian-20" may not be the final name of the aircraft; such information has yet to be released and confirmed.

[3] Craig Covault, "Chinese Test Anti-Satellite Weapon," *Aviation Week*, January 17, 2007. http://www.aviationweek.com/aw/generic/story_channel.jsp?channel=space&id=news/CHI01177.xml.

acknowledged the development of a land-based anti-ship ballistic missile (ASBM) in 2008, academic and government sources have both indicated that the United States underestimated the speed of China's ASBM development. U.S. Department of Defense (DoD) officials have assessed that the ASBM reached initial operational capability (IOC) in December 2010, and official Chinese media and Taiwanese sources have reported that the ASBM is now field deployed with PLA missile units.[4] China's fifth-generation fighter, the J-20, was originally projected to begin prototype testing in 2012; however, the United States also underestimated the speed of its development, as the aircraft made its first publicized flight in January 2011.[5]

Particular challenges to accurate predictive assessments on indigenous Chinese military developments include:

- *Information denial and/or deception:*[6] The PRC exercises secrecy over many aspects of its military affairs, and in some instances puts forth false or misleading information. The lack of transparency in the PRC's military modernization has been a frequent complaint of U.S. defense officials in recent years.
- *Underestimation of changes in China's defense-industrial sector:* Once viewed as a bloated and sclerotic industrial sector incapable of adaptation, in the past decade the PRC defense industry has outperformed the expectations of its critics. While it still faces many problems, the Chinese defense industry is far more capable of producing modern weapons platforms than would have been the case in the 1980s or 1990s.
- *Difficulty in understanding the PRC national security decision-making process:* The decision-making processes of the Chinese government are opaque, particularly in regards to military policy and national security issues. The public emergence and/or testing of some indigenous PRC weapons platforms has also revealed apparent problems of poor bureaucratic coordination, and the possibility of a civil-military divide at the top levels of Chinese policymaking.
- *Underestimation of Beijing's threat perceptions:* Many analysts in media, academia, and the government may have failed to fully appreciate the extent to which the Chinese leadership views the United States as a fundamental threat to China's security. These threat perceptions have been inflamed by a number of events in recent years, to include the 1996 Taiwan Straits Crisis and the accidental 1999 bombing of the PRC Embassy Annex in Belgrade by U.S. aircraft.

---

[4] Zhang Han and Huang Jingjing, "New missile 'ready by 2015'," *People's Daily Online*, February 18, 2011. *http://english.peopledaily.com.cn/90001/90776/90786/7292006.html* ; Rich Chang, "China aims new missile types at Taiwan, NSB (National Security Bureau) says," *Taipei Times Online*, March 17, 2011. *http://www.taipeitimes.com/News/front/archives/2011/03/17/2003498376.*

[5] *Jane's All the World's Aircraft*, "CAC J-20", (Englewood, CO: IHS Jane's: Defense & Security Intelligence & Analysis, January 28, 2011).

[6] As defined by authors Roy Godson and James Wirtz, "Denial and Deception (D&D) is a term often used to describe a combination of information objectives that a nation undertakes to achieve its objectives. *Denial* refers to the attempt to block information that could be used by an opponent to learn some truth. *Deception,* by contrast, refers to a nation's effort to cause an adversary to believe something that is not true." Roy Godson and James Wirtz, *Strategic Denial and Deception: the Twenty-First Century Challenge* (Piscataway, NJ: Transaction Publishers, 2009), pp. 1-2. In an on-the-record Department of Defense briefing for the press in October 2001, the terms denial and deception were defined as follows: "Denial is... attempts to deny your adversary key information either about your military forces, your leadership, the status of your country, the effect of the adversary's campaign on your country, on its infrastructure, et cetera, et cetera... Deception is slightly different... if you look at denial as what we would call hiding the real, deception is showing the fake." See "Background Briefing on Enemy Denial and Deception," Office of the Assistant Secretary of Defense (Public Affairs) October 24, 2001. *http://www.defense.gov/transcripts/transcript.aspx?transcriptid=2162*.

- ***China's increased investments in science and technology:*** China's intensive efforts over the past two decades to stimulate its indigenous capabilities for scientific research and development (R&D)—whether through science education, state funding for research, seeking technology transfers from foreign companies, or industrial espionage—have significantly increased its ability to produce more advanced weapons systems. Furthermore, China's increasing knowledge of dual-use technologies (i.e., those with both commercial and military applications) in areas such as electronics has also offered significant cross-over benefits to the defense-industrial sector.
- ***Inadequate capabilities for and/or attention to the exploitation of open-source Chinese language materials:*** Some of the past flaws in analysis on China's weapons program could have been partially corrected by increased attention to open-source materials, particularly in regards to academic technical journals and related publications. Increased attention to the messages in authoritative PRC media and political science publications would also have improved understanding of the worldview of the Chinese leadership.

The trends of past decades are no longer a reliable guide to the performance of China's defense industries. Furthermore, U.S. observers should not take at face value statements from the Chinese government on military policy, as they could either be deceptive, or simply issued by agencies (e.g., the PRC Ministry of Foreign Affairs) that have no real say over military matters. Based on the trends identified in this paper, U.S. analysts and policymakers should expect to see continued advancements in the ability of the PRC to produce modern weapons platforms, and an attendant increase in the operational capabilities of the People's Liberation Army.

Introduction

The People's Republic of China's (PRC) military modernization efforts accelerated in the mid-1990s—largely due to the 1995–96 Taiwan Strait crisis and the U.S. deployment of two aircraft carriers to the vicinity of Taiwan, which underscored China's inability to counter U.S. military power. In response, the Chinese leadership demanded the development of military options for Taiwan scenarios, which included means to prevent U.S. intervention in the event of a cross-strait conflict.[7]

Judging from the public statements of U.S. officials and reports from U.S. government agencies, the modernization and advancement of Chinese military weapons systems over the past decade have consistently developed faster than both U.S. officials and analysts outside of government expected. U.S. officials and analysts have expressed "surprise" at the speed with which China was able to develop indigenous military technology or weapons systems. Vice Admiral David Dorsett, head of U.S. Navy Intelligence from 2008–2011, has stated in reference to China's ASBM program that the United States "[has] been pretty consistent in underestimating the delivery and IOC of Chinese technology, weapon systems. They've entered operational capability quicker [than expected]."[8] U.S. Secretary of Defense Robert Gates acknowledged in January 2011 that U.S. government intelligence analysts have sometimes underestimated the pace of China's military modernization.[9]

Over the past decade, editions of the Department of Defense's *Annual Report to Congress: Military Power of the People's Republic of China* (hereafter referred to as the DoD annual report) have described China's rapid push toward self-sufficiency in weapons procurement, aided significantly in recent years by Russian conventional weapon technology transfers and sales.[10] As a result of China's modernization drive, the country has made significant progress in developing its own indigenous weapons systems.

Throughout the mid-1990s and the early 2000s, China acquired most of its complex modern weapons systems through imports from Russia and Israel.[11] At the same time, the 1991 Gulf War and the 1995–96 Taiwan Strait Crisis spurred Chinese development and testing of advanced weapons systems as a part of its military modernization program and its drive to develop greater capabilities to conduct a successful "active defense" strategy.[12] By the mid-2000s, China had begun to field indigenous weapons and hardware, aided in part by crossover knowledge from the Chinese civilian industry and the broader global economy.[13]

---

[7] Robert S. Ross, "The 1995–1996 Taiwan Strait Confrontation: Coercion, Credibility, and Use of Force," *International Security*, vol. 25, no. 2 (2000).

[8] Transcript of Defense Writers Group roundtable with Vice Admiral David J. Dorsett, deputy chief of Naval Operations for Information Dominance, January 5, 2011.

[9] John Pomfret, "Defense Secretary Gates: U.S. underestimated parts of China's military modernization," *Washington Post*, January 9, 2011. *http://www.washingtonpost.com/wp-dyn/content/article/2011/01/09/AR2011010901068.html*.

[10] As one such example, see Office of the Secretary of Defense, *Annual Report to Congress: Annual Report on the Military Power of the People's Republic of China* (Washington, DC: U.S. Department of Defense, 2004), p. 32.

[11] Office of the Secretary of Defense, *Annual Report to Congress: The Military Power of the People's Republic of China 2005* (Washington, DC: U.S. Department of Defense, 2005), p. 23.

[12] Office of the Secretary of Defense, *Annual Report on the Military Power of the People's Republic of China* (Washington, DC: U.S. Department of Defense, 2003), pp. 18–19; and Office of the Secretary of Defense, *Annual Report to Congress: The Military Power of the People's Republic of China 2005* (Washington, DC: U.S. Department of Defense, 2005), p. 15.

[13] For discussion of the ways in which technology transfer and expertise gained by Chinese civilian manufacturing companies have carried over into the military realm, see James Mulvenon and Rebecca Samm Tyroler-Cooper, *China's Defense Industry on the Path of Reform* (report produced by Defense Group, Inc., on behalf of the U.S.-China Economic and Security Review Commission, October 2009). *http://www.uscc.gov/researchpapers/2009/DGIReportonPRCDefenseIndustry--FinalVersion_10Nov2009.pdf*; and Micah Springut, Stephen Schlaikjer, and David Chen, *China's Program for Science and*

In 2004, China publicly revealed its indigenously designed diesel-electric *Yuan*-class submarine, a vessel whose existence was reportedly unknown until leaked photos emerged on the Chinese Internet.[14] On January 11, 2007, the People's Republic of China successfully tested an ASAT missile that destroyed China's own *Fengyun*-1C (FY-1C) weather satellite. In December 2010, the commander of the U.S. Pacific Command, Admiral Robert Willard, announced that China's *Dongfeng*-21D (DF-21D/CSS-5) ASBM had reached initial operational capacity, suggesting a rapid advancement in China's command of missile and guidance technology over the past decade.[15] In early 2011, leaked photos and test flight footage of China's prototype fifth-generation stealth fighter, the *Jian*-20 (J-20), inspired a deeper investigation by U.S. analysts and media for information on the specific features and capabilities of the aircraft.[16]

Through examination of the development of the four major Chinese military platforms and systems listed below, this report aims to delineate both trends and patterns in Chinese People's Liberation Army military modernization, as well as in U.S. assessments and predictions concerning Chinese military development:

- Type 039A/B/041 (*Yuan*-class) diesel-electric attack submarine
- SC-19 anti-satellite (ASAT) system
- *Dongfeng*-21D (DF-21D/CSS-5) anti-ship ballistic missile
- Chengdu *Jian*-20 (J-20) stealth fighter aircraft

This report examines each of these purported "surprise" military developments in detail, and seeks to provide a clearer picture as to whether or not U.S. officials and analysts have demonstrated a pattern of underestimating the speed and depth of Chinese military development.

The collection of data for this study has relied solely on open sources, primarily from official government documents (e.g., Department of Defense annual reports, Congressional testimonies, Chinese government white papers), as well as information drawn from reputable media or scholarly sources. No effort has been made to check this data or analysis against materials kept within classified channels. The report assumes information and conclusions contained within official public documents and statements by government agencies (such as the DoD) to be authoritative.

Technology Modernization: Implications for American Competitiveness (report produced by CENTRA Technologies on behalf of the U.S.-China Economic and Security Review Commission, April 2011). *http://www.uscc.gov/researchpapers/2011/USCC_REPORT_China%27s_Program_forScience_and_Technology_Modernization.pdf.*

[14] Bill Gertz, "China Sub Buildup," *Inside the Ring*, December 1, 2006. *http://www.gertzfile.com/gertzfile/ring120106.html.*

[15] Andrew Erickson and Gabe Collins, "China Deploys World's First Long-Range, Land-Based 'Carrier Killer': DF-21D Anti-Ship Ballistic Missile (ASBM) Reaches 'Initial Operational Capability' (IOC)," *China SignPost* (洞察中国), no. 14 (December 26, 2010); Andrew Erickson, "China Testing Anti-Ship Ballistic Missile (ASBM); U.S. Preparing Accordingly–Updated With Latest Analysis & Sources.",*http://www.andrewerickson.com/2010/12/china-testing-anti-ship-ballistic-missile-asbm/.*

[16] Vice Admiral Jack Dorsett, director of Naval Intelligence and Deputy Chief of Naval Operations for Information Dominance, has said, "Still, the lack of transparency into what they're doing, the lack of openness, remains a concern for us," and, "I am intrigued by the developments…I am quite interested in the quantities and different types of technology that have been developed that we either didn't expect or we underestimated." Karen Parrish, "Navy Intel Chief Discusses China's Military Advances," *American Forces Press Service*, January 6, 2011. *http://www.defense.gov/news/newsarticle.aspx?id=62346.*

Section 1: The Type 039A/B/041 (*Yuan*-Class) Submarine

The *Yuan*-class diesel-powered attack submarine[17] was first publicly noted in July 2004, when a photograph of the completed submarine emerged on the Chinese Internet.[18] In 2005, the U.S. Department of Defense acknowledged the addition of a new diesel submarine to China's fleet.[19] There are currently four *Yuan* hulls in active service, with a fifth hull undergoing pre-commissioning sea trials and expected to enter service in 2012.[20]

	Significant Dates
2003	No acknowledgment in the DoD annual report of *Yuan*-class submarine development, though it noted a general Chinese PLA Navy (PLAN) focus on improving submarine technology. The report forecasted a fleet consisting of *Ming, Song,* and *Kilo* attack submarine (SS) class submarines by 2010.[21]
2004	In July, China launches its first new *Yuan*-class submarine.
2004	First public reference to *Yuan*-class submarine in U.S. sources.
2004	DoD notes that PRC submarines blend western and indigenous features and have "several features that point to a major shift in diesel submarine design philosophy."[22]
2006	First *Yuan*-class submarine estimated to have entered service.
2007	Second and third *Yuan*-class submarine launched.
2008	Fourth *Yuan*-class submarine launched.
2009	Second and third *Yuan*-class submarines enter service. U.S. intelligence reports that Yuan submarines may have air-independent propulsion (AIP) capability.[23]
2010	Fourth *Yuan*-class submarine enters service, the fourth of which is a potential redesign of previous versions and incorporates *Kilo*-class features and AIP technology.
2010	China State Shipbuilding Corporation displays AIP technology.[24]
2011	Fifth *Yuan* submarine delivered, conducting sea trials in Shanghai.[25]
2011	Projected date for serial production.[26]

---

[17] There is disagreement among analysts on the proper designation of this submarine. For a brief discussion on the topic, see Ronald O'Rourke, *China's Naval Modernization: Implications for U.S. Navy Capabilities—Background and Issues for Congress*, (Washington, DC: CRS [Congressional Research Service] Report RL33153, December 23, 2010, p. 10.

[18] Lyle Goldstein and William Murray, "China emerges as a maritime power," *Jane's Intelligence Review* (Englewood, CO: IHS Jane's: Defense & Security Intelligence & Analysis, October 1, 2004).

[19] Office of the Secretary of Defense, *Annual Report to Congress: The Military Power of the People's Republic of China 2005* (Washington, DC: U.S. Department of Defense, 2005), p. 33.

[20] Ronald O'Rourke, *China's Naval Modernization: Implications for U.S. Navy Capabilities—Background and Issues for Congress*, (Washington, DC: CRS [Congressional Research Service] Report RL33153, July 22, 2011, p. 24.

[21] Office of the Secretary of Defense, *Annual Report on the Military Power of the People's Republic of China* (Washington, DC: U.S. Department of Defense, 2003), p. 26.

[22] Office of the Secretary of Defense, *Annual Report on the Military Power of the People's Republic of China* (Washington, DC: U.S. Department of Defense, 2004), p. 40.

[23] Office of Naval Intelligence, *The People's Liberation Army Navy: A Modern Navy with Chinese Characteristics* (Suitland, MD: Office of Naval Intelligence, August 2009), p. 23; Office of the Secretary of Defense, *Annual Report to Congress: Military Power of the People's Republic of China 2009* (Washington, DC: U.S. Department of Defense, 2009), p. 49.

[24] Andrei Chang and John Wu, "China Introduces AIP Technology," *Kanwa Defence Review*, December 18, 2010.

[25] Feng, "Activities around Chinese shipyards," *Information Dissemination*, February 5, 2011. *http://www.informationdissemination.net/2011/02/activities-around-chinese-shipyards.html*.

[26] *Jane's Fighting Ships*, "Yuan class (Type 041), Submarines – Patrol submarines, China", (Englewood, CO: IHS Jane's: Defense & Security Intelligence & Analysis, February 11, 2011).

The History and Development of *Yuan*-Class Submarines

Prior to designing and implementing domestic submarines, China imported a majority of its submarine technology from Russia. The first indigenous diesel submarine, the *Ming*-class, was first launched in 1971; it was based on the Soviet *Romeo*-class submarine. The second domestically designed submarine, the *Song*-class, was first launched in 1994. China also bought Russian-designed *Kilo*-class submarines throughout the 1990s and 2000s. The *Yuan*-class submarines (Figure 1) share characteristics of both Russian *Kilo*-class and Chinese indigenous submarines (e.g., *Song*-class)[27] and "are armed similarly to the Song-class SS."[28]

Figure 1: A PLA Navy *Yuan*-class submarine moored pierside.
Source: "Yuan Class (Type 041)," *Jane's Fighting Ships*, entry dated Feb. 11, 2011.

In 2008, DoD assessed the *Yuan*-class submarine to be in "full production" and that it would "be ready for service by 2010."[29] Between 2005 and 2010, the DoD PLA annual report showed a net increase of four diesel submarines, which are likely comprised of a mix between new *Yuan*-, *Song*-, and *Kilo*-class submarines.[30] Over the past decade, China has paid considerable attention to enhancing its submarine fleet. As of the 2009 DoD report, China had over 60 submarines in service (see Figure 2).[31] Series production of the *Yuan*-class submarine is expected, and some analysts predict that "twenty of [the] class [will] be built."[32]

---

[27] *Jane's Underwater Warfare Systems,* "Type 041 (Yuan class) (China), Submarines—Submarine and submersible designs" (Englewood, CO: IHS Jane's: Defense & Security Intelligence & Analysis, August 26, 2010); and Lyle Goldstein and William Murray, "China Emerges as a Maritime Power," *Jane's Intelligence Review* (Englewood, CO: IHS Jane's: Defense & Security Intelligence & Analysis, October 1, 2004).

[28] U.S. Department of Defense, Office of the Secretary of Defense, *Military and Security Developments Involving the People's Republic of China 2010* (Washington, DC: U.S. Government Printing Office), p. 5.

[29] Office of the Secretary of Defense, *Annual Report to Congress: Military Power of the People's Republic of China 2008* (Washington, DC: U.S. Department of Defense, 2008), p. 4.

[30] In determining the new diesel submarines, the author cross-referenced data from the 2005–2010 DoD annual reports and launch dates of new Chinese submarines from 2005 to 2010, as provided by *Jane's*.

[31] Office of the Secretary of Defense, *Annual Report to Congress: Military Power of the People's Republic of China 2009* (Washington, DC: U.S. Department of Defense, 2009), p. 49.

[32] Ronald O'Rourke, *China's Naval Modernization: Implications for U.S. Navy Capabilities—Background and Issues for Congress* (Washington, DC: CRS Report RL33153, April 16, 2010).

Figure 2: Increase in modern naval vessels within the PLA Navy in 2000, 2004, 2008, and 2009. Numbers for submarines (aggregate for both nuclear and diesel-electric propulsion) are shown in the second column from left.

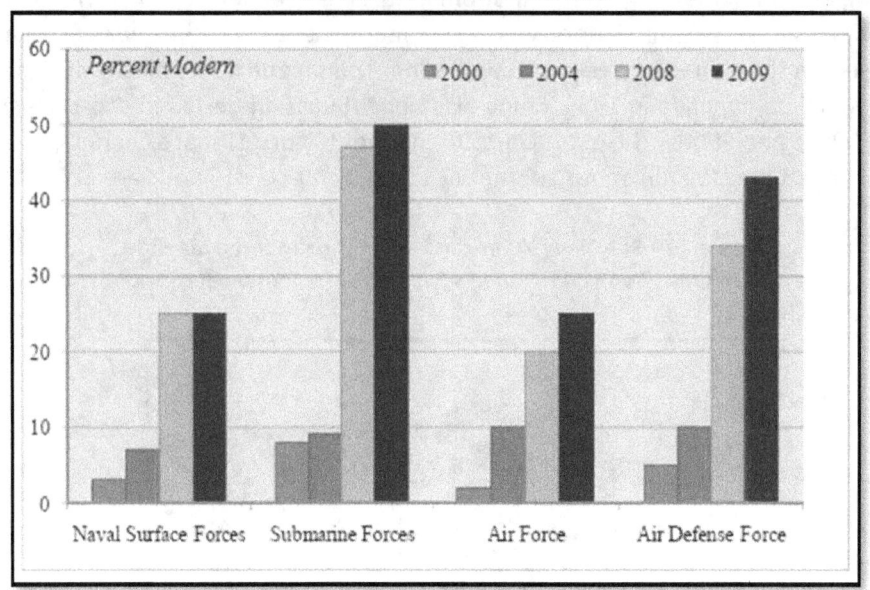

Source: Office of the Secretary of Defense, 2010 Report to Congress.

The current number of Yuan submarines in service is not confirmed, although as of this writing there are at least four commissioned submarines in service (see Table 1, below).

Table 1: Actively Commissioned *Yuan*-Class Submarine Hulls

Number	Builders	Launched	Commissioned
330	Wuhan Shipyard	May 13, 2004	2006
331	Wuhan Shipyard	August 31, 2007	2009
332	Wuhan Shipyard	November 2007	2009
333	Wuhan Shipyard	April 2008	2010

Source: Jane's Fighting Ships, "Yuan class (Type 041)" (Englewood, CO: IHS Jane's: *Defense & Security Intelligence & Analysis*, February 11, 2011).

The 2006 DoD annual report argued that the acquisition and development of new submarines "illustrate[d] the importance the PLA is placing on undersea warfare in its pursuit of sea denial."[33] The 2008 report reiterated this concern, arguing that the increased presence of advanced submarines "reflect[s] Beijing's desire to protect and advance its maritime interests up to and beyond the second island chain."[34] Many members of the U.S. Congress have also expressed concern regarding China's modernization of its submarine fleet, including Senator Jim Webb (VA) and Representative Duncan Hunter (CA–52nd Dist.).[35]

---

[33] Office of the Secretary of Defense, *Annual Report to Congress Military Power of the People's Republic of China 2006* (Washington, DC: U.S. Department of Defense, 2006), p. 26.

[34] The second island chain consists of the islands extending south and east from Japan, to and beyond Guam in the western Pacific Ocean. Office of the Secretary of Defense, *Annual Report to Congress: Military Power of the People's Republic of China 2008* (Washington, DC: U.S. Department of Defense, 2008), p. 29.

[35] Senate Committee on Foreign Relations, Subcommittee on East Asian and Pacific Affairs, *Hearing on Maritime Disputes and Sovereignty Issues in East Asia*, 111th Cong., 1st sess., July 15, 2009; and House of Representatives, Committee on Ways and

In March 2007, *Jane's Navy International* reported that the *Yuan*-class submarine hulls were rumored to have air-independent propulsion (AIP) capability. AIP capability allows a diesel-propulsion submarine to remain submerged for up to several weeks, decreasing its chances of detection.[36] In 2009, both the Office of Naval Intelligence (ONI) as well as the 2009 DoD annual report on China speculated that the *Yuan*-class could be equipped with an AIP system.[37] The full extent of AIP system integration into the Yuan-class submarine fleet is unknown. However, China Shipbuilding & Offshore Co. Ltd.'s recently brokered deal with Pakistan jointly to design and build six AIP-equipped submarines alludes to China's proficiency in AIP capability.[38]

By 2007, it became clear that DoD and other agencies were paying increased attention to China's submarine fleet and particularly to the increase in attack submarines in the PLAN's order of battle. The DoD report on China's military from that year also noted that China had become "capable of serial production of modern diesel-electric submarines."[39]

Factors Affecting Analysis on the Development of the *Yuan*-Class Submarine

Challenge #1: Chinese Efforts at Information Denial

The extent of the "surprise" factor in the launch of the *Yuan* submarine class is subject to debate. In 2004, Bill Gertz of *The Washington Times* asserted that U.S. intelligence was caught off guard by the development of the Yuan-class submarine.[40] *Jane's Underwater Warfare Systems* posited that the emergence of the Yuan submarine "came as a surprise to Western intelligence analysts."[41] Chinese media also alleged that the U.S. government underestimated the development of the submarine.[42]

Critics have noted that Chinese open source materials featured discussion and debates on the development of new diesel submarines and technologies such as AIP,[43] and that analysts who tracked

Means, Subcommittee on Trade, *Hearing on Legislation Related to Trade With China*, 2 August 2007, 110th Cong., 1st sess., August 2, 2007.

[36] *Jane's Underwater Warfare Systems*, "Type 041 (Yuan class) (China), Submarines—Submarine and submersible designs" (Englewood, CO: IHS Jane's: Defense & Security Intelligence & Analysis, August 26, 2010); He Fan, "Foreign Media: Two 'Yuan' Class Submarines To Enter Service in Next Two Years: Military Experts: Combining Russian and European Advanced Technology, Comprehensive Combat Effectiveness Enhanced," *Wen Wei Po* Online (Chinese), October 12, 2010. OSC ID: CPP20101012787016.

[37] Office of Naval Intelligence, *The People's Liberation Army Navy: A Modern Navy with Chinese Characteristics* (Suitland, MD: Office of Naval Intelligence, August 2009), p. 23; Office of the Secretary of Defense, *Annual Report to Congress: Military Power of the People's Republic of China 2009* (Washington, DC: U.S. Department of Defense, 2009), p. 49.

[38] Usman Ansari, "Pakistan in Deal To Buy Chinese Subs: Report," *Defense* News, March 14, 2011. http://www.defensenews.com/story.php?i=5950214&c=FEA&s=CVS.

[39] Office of the Secretary of Defense, *Annual Report to Congress: Military Power of the People's Republic of China 2007* (Washington, DC: U.S. Department of Defense, 2007), p. 27.

[40] Bill Gertz, "Chinese Produce New Type of Sub," *Washington Times*, July 16, 2004, http://www.washingtontimes.com/news/2004/jul/16/20040716-123134-8152r.

[41] *Jane's Underwater Warfare Systems*, "Type 041 (Yuan class) (China), Submarines—Submarine and submersible designs," (Englewood, CO: IHS Jane's: Defense & Security Intelligence & Analysis, August 26, 2010).

[42] Ni Eryan, "The Point of the Military is to Prevent Violence—Unconfirmed Reports Convey Real Information," Hong Kong *Wen Wei Po* Online (Chinese), January 10, 2011. OSC ID: CPP20110110787012.

[43] Jeffrey Lewis, "Yuan Class Submarine," *Arms Control Wonk*, June 10, 2005. http://lewis.armscontrolwonk.com/archive/639/yuan-class-submarine.

the discourse in these sources should not have been surprised. The 2002 DoD annual report implied the intelligence community's awareness of the incorporation of AIP on newer submarines.[44] Thus, another surprise—aside from the sudden appearance of this new class of ship—may have been the pace of development or extent of modifications on existing submarine technology that went into the design of the *Yuan*.

Open source reporting on the *Yuan*-class submarine program continues to be limited. A lack of Chinese government and military transparency is a primary reason the United States could not accurately predict and expect the development of the Yuan submarine. Official PRC statements on the force structure and operations of China's submarine forces are scarce, and references are vague. The development of the *Yuan*-class submarine may have remained secret due to the fact that it was built "completely underground in a secret Chinese production facility that included underground waterways to a port," although the U.S. government has not confirmed this.[45] The secrecy surrounding the *Yuan* program is therefore a good example of the "denial" part of what the U.S. government terms "denial and deception": the effort to keep national security-related information hidden from potential adversaries.[46]

Challenge #2: Changes in the Capabilities of the PRC Defense-Industrial Sector

Another challenge to accurate analysis of the *Yuan* submarine program may have been an underestimation of the extent of changes in the Chinese defense industry in the 1990s and early 2000s, and thereby of the emerging ability of the PRC to produce more advanced indigenous weapons systems. Earlier commentary in the United States tended to look askance on the PRC defense industry as a sclerotic sector poorly capable of reforming itself. One example of such thinking may be seen in a 2001 article from *U.S. News and World Report*, which stated that

> *China, with a decrepit industrial base and a risk-averse socialist bureaucracy, faces even more difficulty than advanced nations in developing high-tech weaponry... [and] Beijing's Communist leadership appears far more concerned about threats from inside China than about extending its military reach. China also faces a mounting financial crunch. While its economy is growing rapidly, the Chinese government still supports numerous Soviet-style, state-run businesses, which mostly lose money... Meanwhile, Chinese troops appear to be minor leaguers compared with their American counterparts.[47]*

There are a number of reasons why these assumptions were formed and proved resistant to change. In many cases, predictions of continuity based on past observable phenomena prove to be accurate. The PRC defense industry saw little substantive advancement in the 1980s and early 1990s; continued lack of progress and reform was the most obvious assumption to make. However, paradigm shifts can and do occur—catching even experts by surprise—and both individuals and institutions are reluctant to backtrack on issues once they have stated an opinion.[48]

---

[44] Office of the Secretary of Defense, *Annual Report on the Military Power of the People's Republic of China 2002* (Washington, DC: U.S. Department of Defense, 2002), p. 21

[45] Bill Gertz, "China Sub Buildup," *Inside the Ring*, December 1, 2006. *http://www.gertzfile.com/gertzfile/ring120106.html*; Bill Gertz, "Commercial Photos Show Chinese Nuke Buildup," *Washington Times*, February 16, 2006. *http://www.washingtontimes.com/news/2006/feb/16/20060216-020211-7960r/*.

[46] For definitions of the terms "denial" and "deception," see footnote #6.

[47] Richard J. Newman and Kevin Whitelaw, "China: How Big a Threat?" *U.S. News & World Report*, July 23, 2001.

[48] As noted by longtime Defense Intelligence Agency analyst Cynthia Grabo, "there is an inherent great reluctance on the part of many individuals and probably most bureaucratic organizations to stick their necks out on problems which are new, controversial, and above all which could be bad news for higher officials and the policymaker. The effect of these factors and

Research work performed for the Commission in 2009 by Defense Group, Inc. detailed the significant improvements observable in many PRC defense-industrial sectors following reforms instituted in the late 1990s. It also described the crossover benefits that China's defense industry gained from the expansion of export manufacturing in civilian products:

> The relative progress of an individual defense-industrial sector appears to be best explained by its relative integration into the globalized production and R&D chain, which provides access to the latest production and manufacturing technologies and know-how... the greatest progress appears to have been made in the shipbuilding and defense electronics sectors, both of which have benefited greatly from China's current position as a leading producer of commercial ships and information technologies.[49]

The forces of globalized markets, tied to the Chinese government's policies to reform the defense-industrial sector and to draw in the best of foreign manufacturing know-how, have dramatically changed the capabilities of the PRC to produce its own advanced indigenous weapons platforms. These factors may not have been clear to outside analysts in the 1990s, but by the middle of the 2000s they were beginning to bear fruit. These changes are now clearly recognized by analysts with the U.S. Department of Defense:

> Since the late 1990s, China's state-owned defense and defense-related companies have undergone a broad-based transformation. Beijing continues to improve its business practices, streamline bureaucracy, broaden incentives for its factory workers, shorten developmental timelines, improve quality control, and increase overall defense industrial production capacity.[50]

Although many problems remain in the Chinese defense industry,[51] it has moved away from the hidebound bureaucratic structures of the 1970s and 1980s. Although the industry remains firmly under state control,[52] structural reform and technological advancements have made it far more capable of producing modern weapons platforms than would have been the case two decades ago.

---

possibly others, individually and collectively, can be to retard the analysis and acceptance of data in the intelligence system by weeks, months and sometimes even years." Cynthia Grabo, *Anticipating Surprise: Analysis for Strategic Warning* (Washington, DC: Joint Military Intelligence College Center for Strategic Intelligence Research, December 2002), p. 45.

[49] James Mulvenon and Rebecca Samm Tyroler-Cooper, *China's Defense Industry on the Path of Reform* (report prepared on behalf of the U.S.-China Economic and Security Review Commission) Defense Group, Inc. (October 2009), p. 4. http://www.uscc.gov/researchpapers/2009/DGIReportonPRCDefenseIndustry--FinalVersion_10Nov2009.pdf.

[50] *Military and Security Developments Involving the People's Republic of China 2011* (Arlington, VA: U.S. Department of Defense, 2011), pp. 41-42.

[51] Robert Karniol, "China Defense Industry Faces Homemade Engine Troubles," *The Straits Times* (Singapore), July 20, 2011.

[52] The armaments industry is one of seven economic sectors identified as "strategic" by the Chinese government, meaning that the government intends to retain more than 50 percent control of the companies in that sector. See U.S. China Economic and Security Review Commission, *Annual Report to Congress 2007* (Washington, DC: Government Printing Office, 2007), p. 39.

Section 2: The Anti-Satellite (ASAT) Weapon System (SC-19)

On January 11, 2007, China successfully tested a direct-ascent anti-satellite (ASAT) weapon, destroying one of its own weather satellites, the FY-1C, approximately 530 miles above Earth.[53] The test, which produced history's greatest single instance of human-created space debris, provoked U.S. and international concern about space environmental safety and further raised questions regarding the implications of the test for the vulnerability of U.S. satellite systems to adversarial attacks.

The U.S. Government called on China to explain its actions on January 15, although China did not publicly acknowledge the test until January 23. Then, China's Foreign Ministry stated that the test was not directed at any other country and that China had no intention of pursuing the weaponization of space.[54] While this language is consistent with previous public official statements such as those contained within the PRC's defense white papers, the test incited further controversy when China failed to provide explanations to international questions regarding its intentions for the ASAT program[55]—a refusal that has continued to this day.

Significant Dates	
1998	DoD reports to Congress that China is acquiring foreign technologies that could be used to develop an ASAT capability.[56]
2003	DoD reports on China's ASAT ambitions and the "inevitability" of space-based missile defenses. The report is unclear on China's assessed ASAT capability but projects that an ASAT system will be fielded in 2005-2010.[57]
2004	DoD assessed that China is on its way to attaining ASAT capability, with testing estimated to begin in the near future.[58]
2007	On January 11, China conducts successful ASAT weapon test on FY-1C weather satellite.
2007	On January 15, U.S. officials publicly mention China's ASAT test.
2007	Following earlier evasive statements, on January 23 China's Foreign Ministry makes a pro forma public statement acknowledging the ASAT test, stating that "[t]his test was not directed at any country and does not constitute a threat to any country."[59]
2010	On January 11, China launches SC-19 missile to destroy CSS-X-11 medium-range ballistic missile (MRBM) in space.[60]

---

[53] For more details on the ASAT test, see Shirley Kan, *China's Anti-Satellite Weapon Test* (Washington, DC: CRS Report RS22652, April 23, 2007). For more on China's space program and military space strategy, see the forthcoming transcript for the U.S.-China Economic and Security Commission's May 11, 2011, hearing, "China's Space Advances." See as well as the forthcoming report on China's space program produced on behalf of the Commission by the Project 2049 Institute, expected to be released in autumn 2011.

[54] Joseph Kahn, "China Shows Assertiveness in Weapons Test," *New York Times*, January 20, 2007. *http://www.nytimes.com/2007/01/20/world/asia/20china.html.*

[55] Tim Ross and Holly Watt, "WikiLeaks: US vs China in battle of the anti-satellite space weapons," *Telegraph* (London), February 2, 2011.

[56] Report to Congress pursuant to Section 1226 of the Fiscal Year 1998 National Defense Authorization Act, *Future Military Capabilities and Strategy of the People's Republic of China* (Washington, DC: Department of Defense, November 1998).

[57] Office of the Secretary of Defense, *Annual Report to Congress: Military Power of the People's Republic of China 2003* (Washington, DC: U.S. Department of Defense, 2003), p. 9.

[58] Office of the Secretary of Defense, *Annual Report on the Military Power of the People's Republic of China 2004* (Washington, DC: U.S. Department of Defense, 2004), p. 42.

[59] James Mulvenon, "Rogue Warriors: A Puzzled Look at the Chinese ASAT Test," *China Leadership Monitor*, no. 20 (Winter 2007).

[60] Holly Watt, "WikiLeaks: timeline of the space race," *Telegraph* (London), February 2, 2011.

History and Development of ASAT Capability

China's rapidly developing aerospace capability signifies a critical shift in the military and strategic environment in U.S.-China and international relations. Chinese R&D on fundamental ASAT technologies can be traced to the 1960s.[61] Open source evidence suggests that preliminary research on ASAT technologies (e.g., ground-based directed energy lasers, terminal guidance systems, and satellite jamming) began in the 1980s[62] and that the PLA has been "developing ASAT weapons as a national priority since at least the early 1990s."[63] There is also evidence that Chinese researchers have espoused the systematic study and analysis of military satellites in order better to take "countermeasure techniques against satellite reconnaissance."[64]

Figure 3: Artist's Conception of China's Anti-Satellite Test

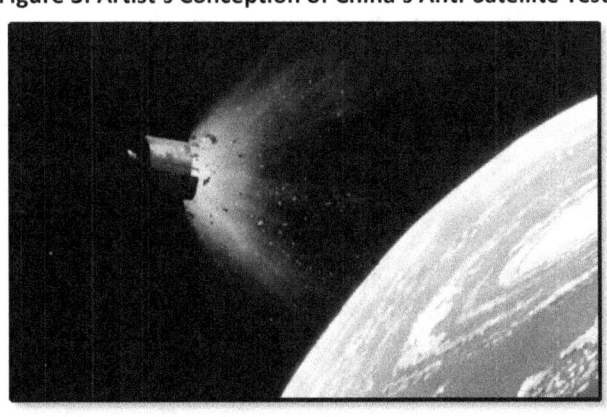

Source: Discover, "Space Junk: How to Clean Up the Space Age's Mess."

In 1998, the Secretary of Defense William Cohen made a public reference to China's development of ASAT weapons;[65] however, some analysts still expressed doubts.[66] As of the early 2000s, many subscribed to the skeptical argument of defense journalist Theresa Hitchens that

> *There is little evidence to date that any other country...possesses both the mature technology and the intention to seriously threaten American military or commercial operations in space—and even less evidence of serious pursuit of actual space-based weapons by potentially hostile actors. There are severe technical barriers and high costs to overcome for all but the most rudimentary ASAT capabilities, especially for development of on-orbit weapons. It further remains unclear what political drivers—outside of American development of space-based weaponry—would force American competitors, in the near- to medium-term to seriously pursue such technology.[67]*

---

[61] Federation of American Scientists, "Chinese Anti-Satellite [ASAT] Capabilities," June 23, 2000. *http://www.fas.org/spp/guide/china/military/asat/.*

[62] Mark Stokes, *China's Strategic Modernization: Implications for the United States,* September 1999, pp. 118–121.

[63] Ian Easton, "The Great Game in Space: China's Evolving ASAT Weapons Programs and Their Implications for Future U.S. Strategy" (Arlington, VA: *Project 2049 Institute,* 2009), p. 2.

[64] Que Wenyan and Yang Bo, "Radar Countermeasure Techniques Against Satellite Reconnaissance," *Xiandai Leida,* February 1, 2004. OSC ID: CPP20041202000209.

[65] U.S. Department of Defense, Office of the Secretary of Defense, "Future Military Capabilities and Strategy of the People's Republic of China" (Washington, DC: Department of Defense, 1998).

[66] Shirley Kan, *China's Anti-Satellite Weapon Test* (Washington, DC: CRS Report RL22652, April 23, 2007), p. 2.

[67] Theresa Hitchens, "Monsters and Shadows: Left Unchecked, American Fears Regarding Space Assets Will Drive Weaponization," *Disarmament Forum,* no. 1 (2003): 22.

There have also been debates on the development—and potential dual use—of China's space program, including whether it would be used to boost national prestige or to reinforce the PLA's space warfare strategy.[68] Such a strategy could be summarized as creating and maintaining a favorable security environment through credible deterrence and, in the event of actual military conflict, the ability to conduct modern, high-tech joint campaigns involving operations in outer space.[69] Indeed, at the time, China was believed to lack a number of capabilities that would be required for a viable ASAT program, leading analysts outside of government to conclude that Beijing's "ultimate commitment to developing ASAT weapons remains ambiguous."[70]

China's repeated calls for peaceful use of space and expressed concerns regarding space debris indicated opposition to counterspace and space deterrence programs; however, Chinese technical papers and the 2007 ASAT test proved that its intentions were otherwise.[71] The 2007 ASAT test, therefore, was a political "surprise" to those who accepted the PRC's official position at face value, but it was not unexpected by the U.S. intelligence and policy community. The ASAT test brought to public attention the fact that China could execute capabilities that undermine or complicate U.S. access to space in the event of a conflict.

However, U.S. government analysts were tracking Chinese ASAT development at least as early as 2003: the Department of Defense's annual report on Chinese military power for that year acknowledged that China was developing and planned to field a direct-ascent ASAT system.[72] Subsequent DoD annual reports have noted China's capability to "destroy or disable satellites...by launching a ballistic missile or space-launch vehicle armed with a nuclear weapon." [73] The 2006 report described China as pursuing an "offensive anti-satellite system" and ground-based ASAT weapons systems.[74] Between September 2004 and January 2007, China conducted a total of four direct-ascent ASAT tests, all of which were known to U.S. analysts.[75]

DoD annual reports released after the 2007 ASAT test indicated an increased focus on the possibility of future Chinese tests, as well as on the military and counterspace applications of ASAT technology.[76]

[68] Phillip Saunders et al., *China's Space Capabilities and the Strategic Logic of Anti-Satellite Weapons*, July 22, 2002. http://cns.miis.edu/stories/020722.htm.

[69] For a discussion of China's space strategy, see Office of the Secretary of Defense, *Military Power of the People's Republic of China* (Washington, DC: U.S. Department of Defense, 2007), p. 21; M. Taylor Fravel, "The Evolution of China's Military Strategy," in *China's Revolution in Doctrinal Affairs: Emerging Trends in the Operational Art of the Chinese People's Liberation Army,* eds. James Mulvenon and David Finkelstein (Alexandria, VA: The CNA Corporation, 2005), pp. 96–97; Dean Cheng, "Zhanyixue and Joint Campaigns," in *China's Revolution in Doctrinal Affairs: Emerging Trends in the Operational Art of the Chinese People's Liberation Army,* eds. James Mulvenon and David Finkelstein (Alexandria, VA: The CNA Corporation, 2005), pp. 109–110; and Ashley J. Tellis, "China's Military Space Strategy," *Survival* 49, no. 3 (2007): 41–72.

[70] Phillip Saunders et al., *China's Space Capabilities and the Strategic Logic of Anti-Satellite Weapons*, July 22, 2002. http://cns.miis.edu/stories/020722.htm.

[71] Eric C. Anderson and Jeffrey G. Engstrom, *China's Use of Perception Management and Strategic Deception* (Washington, DC: U.S.-China Economic and Security Review Commission, November 2009), p. 44.

[72] U.S. Department of Defense, Office of the Secretary of Defense, *Annual Report on the Military Power of the People's Republic of China 2003* (Washington, DC: U.S. Government Printing Office, 2003), p. 36.

[73] U.S. Department of Defense, Office of the Secretary of Defense, *Annual Report to Congress: Military Power of the People's Republic of China 2006* (Washington, DC: U.S. Government Printing Office, 2006), p. 36.

[74] U.S. Department of Defense, Office of the Secretary of Defense, *Annual Report to Congress: Military Power of the People's Republic of China 2006* (Washington, DC: US. Government Printing Office), p. 35.

[75] Ashley J. Tellis, "China's Military Space Strategy," *Survival* 49, no. 3 (2007): 41–72.

[76] Office of the Secretary of Defense, *Military Power of the People's Republic of China 2008* (Washington, DC: U.S. Department of Defense, 2008), pp. 20–21; Office of the Secretary of Defense, *Military Power of the People's Republic of China 2008*

While the United States was aware of Chinese technological and aerospace development (with potential application to ASAT weapons), due to China's stated official stance on outer space, U.S. decisionmakers may not have focused on ASAT developments as closely until after the successful 2007 test.[77]

In 2007, Lieutenant General (LTG) Michael Maples, director of the Defense Intelligence Agency (DIA) testified to Congress that the ASAT test would allow China "to eventually deploy an ASAT system that could threaten U.S. satellites."[78] Later, in 2009, LTG Maples acknowledged that China is developing systems and technologies targeting "U.S. space-based navigation, communication, and intelligence collection capabilities." He argued that China "will continue to deploy more advanced satellites through the next decade," including "developing jammers and kinetic and directed-energy weapons for ASAT missions." LTG Maples also indicated China's dual use of civilian aerospace technologies to improve "its ability to track and identify satellites—a prerequisite for anti-satellite attacks."[79] Others, such as Lieutenant General Wallace Gregson (USMC, ret.), then Assistant Secretary of Defense for Asian and Pacific Security Affairs, have testified that these moves are "just one element of China's military modernization effort[s] to develop and field disruptive military technologies."[80]

With the growing importance of space assets for China's burgeoning military C4ISR infrastructure, the possibility of future ASAT tests is not unexpected. However, it would elicit great international concern for potentially damaging space debris and has immense strategic implications for U.S. space capabilities. The reliance of the United States on space assets for intelligence, surveillance, and reconnaissance; communication; navigation; and positioning creates a particular vulnerability to attacks, and thus the potential consequences of another test or even an offensive strike are grave. It seems likely, however, that the United States will develop its own deterrents to China's newfound counterspace capability.[81]

In any case, it now seems clear that China's intended approach is to continue to develop ground-based kinetic kill vehicles (e.g., the SC-19 ASAT), as well as lasers and a variety of jammers and other electromagnetic spectrum disruption hardware. It is also simultaneously attempting—sometimes in concert with Russia—to limit the space power of the United States and other potential competitor nations by repeatedly proposing arms control agreements that would limit the "weaponization of and an arms race in outer space" by restricting *space*-based platforms, but that would not regulate *ground*-based anti-space platform capabilities.[82]

(Washington, DC: U.S. Department of Defense, 2008), pp. 27–28; Office of the Secretary of Defense, *Military Power of the People's Republic of China 2009* (Washington, DC: U.S. Department of Defense, 2009), pp. 25–27;

[77] Eric C. Anderson and Jeffrey G. Engstrom, *China's Use of Perception Management and Strategic Deception* (Washington, DC: U.S.-China Economic and Security Review Commission, November 2009), pp. 44–45.

[78] Senate Armed Services Committee, "Current and Projected National Security Threats to the United States," Michael Maples, statement for the record, 110th Cong., 1st sess., February 27, 2007.

[79] Senate Armed Services Committee, *Hearing on Current and Future Worldwide Threats to the National Security of the United States*, 111th Cong., 1st sess., March 10, 2009.

[80] Senate Armed Services Committee, *Hearing on Nominations Before the Senate Armed Services Committee*, 111th Cong., 1st sess., April 28, 2009.

[81] Ian Easton, "The Great Game in Space: China's Evolving ASAT Weapons Programs and Their Implications for Future U.S. Strategy (Arlington, VA: Project 2049 Institute, 2009), p. 11.

[82] Ministry of Foreign Affairs of the People's Republic of China, "Prevention of an Arms Race in Outer Space," Press Release, April 7, 2011. *http://www.mfa.gov.cn/eng/wjb/zzjg/jks/kjlc/wkdd/t410757.htm.*

Factors Affecting Analysis on the Development of the Anti-Satellite Missile System

Challenge #1: Strategic Deception and Misleading Messages

The U.S. government did not underestimate China's potential to field ASAT capabilities, nor was it caught off guard by the January 2007 test. However, it is possible that western commentators outside of government (e.g., Hitchens *et al.*) may have been misled by China's public statements concerning the use of weapons in space.[83] China's diplomatic stance and official rhetoric, juxtaposed with its reluctance post-January 2007 to engage with the United States and other foreign countries on addressing military uses of space, created separate "public" and "behind-the-scenes" stances on space militarization.

In its white papers up until 2006, China espoused that outer space should be used exclusively for peaceful purposes and that it was opposed to any militarization of space, including the development of anti-satellite weapons. The papers emphasized utilizing "an international legal instrument" in preventing the weaponization of space.[84] By the publication of its 2006 white paper, however, the "legal instrument" aspect was not mentioned, hinting at possible ASAT development. By the 2008 Defense white paper, however, the term reappeared, which raised questions among the analytical and intelligence community about the motives behind China's words and actions.[85]

When questioned by the international community in early 2007 regarding its ASAT test, PRC spokespersons provided contradictory responses from different branches of its government (i.e., Foreign Ministry as compared to the PLA), which led some observers to speculate that the incident revealed either a rift in policy coordination, or an active effort to deceive the rest of the world regarding China's programs for space weapons.[86]

Scholars who observe China's historical and military philosophy have identified strategic deception as an oft-practiced tactic to manipulate an opponent's strategic assessment process and influence the "highest military authorities responsible for formulating strategic decisions."[87] Perception management, on the other hand, is broadly defined as presenting misinformation with the intent "to influence how other nations perceive Chinese interests and actions."[88] The secretive and nontransparent nature of the Chinese government leaves outside observers unsure as to what extent government pronouncements on China's military modernization should be accepted *prima facie*.[89]

---

[83] Craig Covault, "Chinese Test Anti-Satellite Weapon," *Aviation Week*, January 17, 2007. *http://www.aviationweek.com/aw/generic/story_channel.jsp?channel=space&id=news/CHI01177.xml*; Eric C. Anderson and Jeffrey G. Engstrom, *China's Use of Perception Management and Strategic Deception* (Washington, DC: U.S.-China Economic and Security Review Commission, November 2009).

[84] Information Office of the State Council of the People's Republic of China, *White Paper on China's National Defense*, 1998; Information Office of the State Council of the People's Republic of China, *White Paper on China's National Defense*, 2000; Information Office of the State Council of the People's Republic of China, *White Paper on China's National Defense*, 2004.

[85] Eric C. Anderson and Jeffrey G. Engstrom, *China's Use of Perception Management and Strategic Deception* (Washington, DC: U.S.-China Economic and Security Review Commission, November 2009), p. 44.

[86] James Mulvenon, "Rogue Warriors? A Puzzled Look at the Chinese ASAT Test," *China Leadership Monitor* no. 20 (April 15, 2007): 1.

[87] Yu Qiaohua, "Strategic Deception" [战略欺骗 Zhanlue Qipian], in *Chinese Military Encyclopedia*, ed. Fu Quanyu (Beijing: Military Science Publishing House, 2002), p. 583.

[88] Eric C. Anderson and Jeffrey G. Engstrom, *China's Use of Perception Management and Strategic Deception* (Washington, DC: U.S.-China Economic and Security Review Commission, November 2009), pp. 7–8.

[89] Phillip C. Saunders and Michael Kiselycznyk, "How Transparent is the PLA?" Pacific Forum CSIS *PacNet* no. 30 (June 15, 2010). *http://csis.org/files/publication/pac1030.pdf*.

The selective dissemination of information is a strategy that is also rooted in the "institutional culture and accustomed practices of the Chinese Communist Party," which has "a deeply ingrained tendency toward secretiveness and a long history of proactively using information to promote the party's objectives while suppressing information deemed harmful to its interests."[90] The opaque nature of today's Chinese government and military often makes it difficult to ascertain trends and breakthroughs on military technology and hardware development. China restricts most military and defense-related information from the public, and "many aspects of China's national security policy, including its motivations, intentions, and decision-making processes, remain secret."[91]

Challenge #2: Poor Policy Coordination and a Chinese Civil-Military Divide?

Historically, the PLA has exercised considerable influence in the CCP, and while the civilian leadership technically has control over the PLA, the relationship between PLA commanders and the civilian leadership is complex.[92] Some analysts have argued that gaps in U.S. knowledge of Chinese military developments result in part from poor policy coordination between civilian and military officials in China's central leadership, though the true extent of such a civil-military divide is difficult to determine.[93]

The January 2007 ASAT test provides a prime example of poor bureaucratic coordination. China's Ministry of Foreign Affairs (MFA) took 12 days to publicly confirm the event, a substantially long time given the international response and concern prompted by the ASAT test. This provoked widespread speculation that the MFA was not informed of the launch beforehand.[94] In a similar fashion, President Hu Jintao's expressed surprise at the J-20 test flight during Secretary of Defense Gates' visit to Beijing on January 11, 2011, also led some analysts to posit the existence of a civil-military divide *(see pages 33-34)*.[95] While some analysts and scholars have suggested that the civilian leadership may have been unaware of the ASAT and J-20 tests, other sources indicate that the decision to test the ASAT weapon was carefully deliberated between the civilian and military leadership.[96]

Other analysts, such as Nan Li of the U.S. Naval War College, have argued that the prolonged silence after the 2007 ASAT test was a calculated act "intended to aggravate the sense of uncertainty for China's opponents, thus enhancing the deterrent effect."[97] Dr. Li maintains that post-Deng leaders (i.e., Jiang

---

[90] U.S.-China Economic and Security Review Commission, *2009 Annual Report to Congress* (Washington, DC: U.S. Government Printing Office, November 2009), p. 297.

[91] Office of the Secretary of Defense, *Annual Report to Congress: The Military Power of the People's Republic of China 2005*, (Washington, DC: U.S. Government Printing Office, 2005), p. 7.

[92] Susan Shirk, "Domestic Threats," Chap. 3 in *China: Fragile Superpower* (New York, NY: Oxford University Press, 2007), pp. 70–72.

[93] U.S.-China Economic and Security Review Commission, *Hearing on China's Narratives Regarding National Security Policy*, written testimony of Andrew Scobell, March 10, 2011

[94] James Mulvenon, "Rogue Warriors? A Puzzled Look at the Chinese ASAT Test," *China Leadership Monitor* 20 (April 15, 2007): 1.

[95] Jim Garamone, "Gates: Chinese Taking Strategic Dialogue Proposal Seriously" (Washington, DC: U.S. Department of Defense, January 11, 2011). *http://www.defense.gov/news/newsarticle.aspx?id=62397*; and U.S.-China Economic and Security Review Commission, *Hearing on China's Narratives Regarding National Security Policy*, written testimony of Andrew Scobell, March 10, 2011.

[96] Gregory Kulacki and Jeffrey Lewis, "Understanding China's ASAT Test," Union of Concerned Scientists, October 31, 2008. *http://www.ucsusa.org/nuclear_weapons_and_global_security/international_information/us_china_relations/understanding-chinas-asat.html.*

[97] Nan Li, "Chinese Civil-Military Relations in the Post-Deng Era: Implications for Crisis Management and Naval Modernization," *U.S. Naval War College China Maritime Studies* 4 (January 2010): 24.

Zemin and Hu Jintao) intentionally created a separation between civil and military realms, confining the PLA to military-technical tasks and externally oriented missions.[98] Dr. Li argues that the doctrinal shift resulted in a barrier between the PLA and domestic politics and that the resulting civil-military bifurcation complicated interagency cooperation, especially in managing both domestic and foreign policy crises (such as the response to the 2007 ASAT test).[99] Open source reporting lends itself to validate all of the above theories, but the extent of a civilian-military divide in policy coordination remains unclear.

Challenge #3: Underestimation of Beijing's Threat Perceptions

PRC behavior surrounding the ASAT program could also be motivated by perceptions of the threat the United States poses to China. Since the United States is the leading military power in space combat, Chinese analysts tend to view the United States as a hostile actor threatening other countries' civilian and military space assets through its insistence on maintaining space dominance, thus driving an international space race where China is forced to respond by developing its own space deterrents.[100]

Alternatively, China may have been motivated to intensify development of military applications for space when U.S. policymakers opposed any measures to curtail space development activity and PAROS (Prevention of an Arms Race in Outer Space).[101] Chinese analysts have argued that China, feeling threatened by the U.S. stance on space and PAROS, may have felt compelled to address the potential security risks with development of ASAT systems.[102]

(For further discussion of PRC threat perceptions in the context of the development of an anti-ship ballistic missile, see pages 26-28 of this report.)

---

[98] Nan Li, "Chinese Civil-Military Relations in the Post-Deng Era: Implications for Crisis Management and Naval Modernization," *U.S. Naval War College China Maritime Studies* 4 (January 2010): 5, 12.

[99] Nan Li, "Chinese Civil-Military Relations in the Post-Deng Era: Implications for Crisis Management and Naval Modernization," *U.S. Naval War College China Maritime Studies* 4 (January 2010): 40.

[100] Zhang Hui, "Space Weaponization and Space Security: A Chinese Perspective," *China Security* no. 2 (2006): 24–36.

[101] NTI, "China's Attitude Toward Outer Space Weapons." *http://www.nti.org/db/china/spacepos.htm*; and Peter B. de Selding, "China Urges U.N. Ban On Space Weaponry," *Space News*, March 22, 1999, pp. 1, 19.

[102] Shixiu Bao, "Deterrence Revisited: Outer Space," *China Security* no. 5 (2007).

Section 3: The Anti-Ship Ballistic Missile (ASBM) (DF-21D/CSS-5)

Chinese naval modernization efforts—including anti-ship ballistic missile development, among the numerous projects and weapons acquisition programs—began in the 1990s. Conventional ballistic missile technology has developed at remarkable speed. The *Dong Feng-21* (DF-21) medium-range ballistic missile, for instance, has several variants.[103] The development of the DF-21D variant (a ground-based ASBM) is reportedly fitted with a maneuverable reentry vehicle (MaRV), has GPS- and active radar-based terminal guidance, and the ability to strike 1,500 to 2,000 kilometers away from China's shores.

Significant Dates

2002	December 19, successful test flight of the terminally guided DF-21C MRBM.[104]
2003	First mention of the CSS-5 MRBM in DoD annual report.[105]
2004	*The Science of Second Artillery Campaigns* book details potential operational uses for an ASBM.
2006	The Office of Naval Intelligence references China's interest in developing an ASBM.[106]
2008	The Defense Intelligence Agency acknowledges China's development of an ASBM.
2008	First mention of the ASBM in DoD annual report.[107]
2009	DF-21D variant constructed, initial operational capability estimated at 2012.[108]
2010	On August 3, private sector analysts estimate the initial operational capability (IOC) of an ASBM to be "a ways off." [109]
2010	In December, Admiral Willard (Commander, U.S. Pacific Command) announces that China's ASBM has reached IOC.
2011	On February 18, Chinese media reports that the ASBM is "already deployed in the army." [110]
2011	General Chen Bingde (Director, PLA General Staff Dept.) publicly confirms that the ASBM is in development.[111]

The History and Development of the ASBM

The origin of the DF-21 missile dates to 1965, when then Chinese Premier Zhou Enlai proposed the development of solid-propellant rocket technology.[112] By 1975, development of a land-based MRBM

---

[103] Mark Stokes, *China's Evolving Conventional Strategic Strike Capability* (Arlington, VA: Project 2049 Institute, September 14, 2009).

[104] Mark Stokes, *China's Evolving Conventional Strategic Strike Capability* (Arlington, VA: Project 2049 Institute, September 14, 2009).

[105] Office of the Secretary of Defense, *Annual Report on the Military Power of the People's Republic of China 2003* (Washington, DC: U.S. Government Printing Office, 2003), p. 29.

[106] U.S. Department of the Navy, *Seapower Questions on the Chinese Submarine Force* (Washington, DC: Office of Naval Intelligence, December 20, 2006).

[107] Office of the Secretary of Defense, *Annual Report to Congress: Military Power of the People's Republic of China 2008* (Washington, DC: U.S. Department of Defense, 2008), pp. I, 2.

[108] Mark Stokes, *China's Evolving Conventional Strategic Strike Capability* (Arlington, VA: Project 2049 Institute, September 14, 2009), p. 3.

[109] Mark Stokes and Tiffany Ma, "Second Artillery Anti-Ship Ballistic Missile Brigade Facilities Under Construction in Guangdong?," *AsiaEye*, August 3, 2010.

[110] Zhang Han and Huang Jingjing, "New missile 'ready by 2015'," *People's Daily* Online, February 18, 2011. *http://english.peopledaily.com.cn/90001/90776/90786/7292006.html.*

[111] Embassy of the People's Republic of China in the United States of America, "陈炳德：东风 21D 导弹还在研究中 [Chen Bingde: Dongfeng 21D Daodan Hai Zai Yanjiu Zhong]," July 11, 2011, *http://www.china-embassy.org/chn/zmqx/t838436.htm*

[112] *SinoDefence*, "DongFeng 21 (CSS-5) Medium-Range Ballistic Missile," June 4, 2010. *http://www.sinodefence.com/strategic/missile/df21.asp.*

designated as "DF-21" was underway. Several variants have since been constructed, each with newer capabilities, increased range, and higher payload.

In 2008, a reference to a developmental Chinese ASBM first appeared in the DoD annual report, although no projections were made regarding its capability or predicted IOC.[113] The 2009 DoD annual report acknowledged the development of an ASBM, its basic characteristics, and the impact it could have on U.S. forces. The 2010 report, however, omitted previously mentioned information on the missile. Although it is clear that U.S. government analysts were aware of Chinese development of ASBM technology, there were no official, unclassified projections for the development of the weapons system.

However, by December 2010 Admiral Willard stated that China's ASBM had reached IOC. On January 5, 2011, Vice Admiral Dorsett, Deputy Chief of Naval Operations for Information Dominance, also stated that the ASBM had reached IOC.[114] On February 18, 2011, Chinese media reported that the ASBM "is already deployed in the army," though this claim has yet to be confirmed by Chinese or U.S. government officials.[115] On March 17, 2011, Taiwanese media reported that National Security Bureau Director Tsai Der-sheng claimed the PLA had already fielded the ASBM, but Chinese Nationalist Party (KMT) Legislator Lin Yu-fang expressed doubts over the assertion.[116] While there is not yet any U.S. confirmation regarding the field deployment of the ASBM, Chief of Naval Operations Admiral Gary Roughead stated in a January 14, 2011, interview that "[i]t would not surprise me that in the next couple of years that the capability will be in play."[117]

A land-based ASBM equipped with maneuverable reentry vehicles is designed to hit mobile surface ships such as aircraft carriers *(a conceptual flight path is illustrated in Figure 4)*. As aircraft carriers are a centerpiece of U.S. naval operations, U.S. analysts and officials understand this to be a particularly disruptive threat: the U.S. Navy has never faced the prospect of ballistic missiles capable of effectively hitting mobile targets at sea.[118]

China has tested the DF-21D missile system over land but not over water against maneuvering targets.[119] Nevertheless, China has extensively researched terminal guidance technologies, possibly to include the guidance employed by the U.S. Pershing II theater ballistic missile with a maneuverable reentry vehicle.[120]

---

[113] Office of the Secretary of Defense, *Annual Report to Congress: Military Power of the People's Republic of China 2008* (Washington, DC: U.S. Department of Defense, 2008), p. 2.

[114] Transcript of Defense Writers Group roundtable with Vice Admiral David J. Dorsett, deputy chief of Naval Operations for Information Dominance, January 5, 2011.

[115] Zhang Han and Huang Jingjing, "New missile 'ready by 2015'," *People's Daily* Online, February 18, 2011. *http://english.peopledaily.com.cn/90001/90776/90786/7292006.html.*

[116] Rich Chang, "China aims new missile types at Taiwan, NSB says," *Taipei Times* Online, March 17, 2011. *http://www.taipeitimes.com/News/front/archives/2011/03/17/2003498376.*

[117] Ronald O'Rourke, *China's Naval Modernization: Implications for U.S. Navy Capabilities—Background and Issues for Congress* (Washington, DC: Congressional Research Service, CRS Report RL33153, February 3, 2011), p. 65.

[118] Senate Committee on Foreign Relations, Subcommittee on East Asian and Pacific Affairs, *Hearing on Maritime Disputes and Sovereignty Issues in East Asia*, 111th Cong., 1st sess., July 15, 2009.

[119] Transcript of Defense Writers Group roundtable with Vice Admiral David J. Dorsett, deputy chief of Naval Operations for Information Dominance, January 5, 2011.

[120] Fan Hangmu, "Satellite-Missile Attack: Exploring a Model for Anti-Ship Ballistic Missile Combat Operations," *Modern Ships (Xiandai Jianchuan)* (November 2010): 30–33. OSC ID: CPP20110118318001; for analysis on Chinese ASBM literature, see Andrew Erickson and David Yang, "Using the Land to Control the Sea? Chinese Analysts Consider the Anti-Ship Ballistic Missile," *Naval War College Review*, vol. 62, no. 4 (Autumn 2009): 53–86.

Figure 4: The Flight Path of a DF-21D Missile

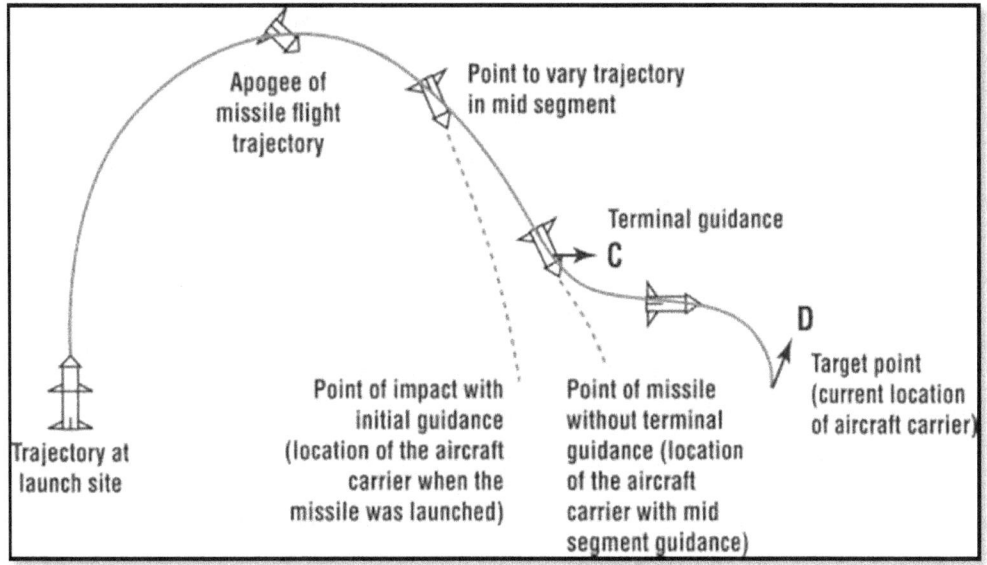

Source: Office of the Secretary of Defense, *Military Power of the People's Republic of China 2009, Annual Report to Congress*, p. 21.

As some experts have projected, it could be years before an ASBM reaches full operational capability. In terms of projections for fielding the ASBM, a September 2009 report by Mark Stokes on China's ASBM program estimated that:

- The initial phase of the program was intended to have a rudimentary 1,500 to 2,000 kilometer range ASBM capability by the end of the 11th Five-Year Plan in 2010.
- A second phase would seek to extend these capabilities out to a range of 3,000 kilometers and enhance aerodynamic maneuvering capabilities by the conclusion of the 12th Five-Year Plan in 2015.
- A third phase would focus on extending conventional precision strike capability out to 8,000 kilometers (intercontinental) before the end of the 13th Five-Year Plan in 2020.
- A final phase would involve global precision strike capability by the conclusion of the 14th Five-Year Plan in 2025.[121]

Aside from the missile, numerous documents indicate significant developments regarding infrastructure and support systems for the ASBM program. This includes the completion of a DF-21D rocket motor facility in 2009, and the launching of co-orbital electric intelligence satellites and remote sensing satellites that could be used to provide imagery of China's maritime periphery and support long-range precision strikes.[122]

---

[121] Mark Stokes, *China's Evolving Conventional Strategic Strike Capability* (Arlington, VA: Project 2049 Institute, September 14, 2009), p. 10.

[122] U.S. Department of Defense, Office of the Secretary of Defense, *Military and Security Developments Involving the People's Republic of China 2010* (Washington, DC: U.S. Government Printing Office), p. 2; Mark Stokes, *China's Evolving Conventional Strategic Strike Capability* (Arlington, VA: Project 2049 Institute, September 14, 2009), p. 3; Andrew Erickson, "Satellites Support Growing PLA Maritime Monitoring and Targeting Capabilities," *China Brief* 11, no. 3 (February 10, 2011). *http://www.jamestown.org/single/?no_cache=1&tx_ttnews[tt_news]=37490.*; Ian Easton, "China's Secret Co-orbital Satellites:

While reaching IOC is a significant achievement, sources suggest that obstacles remain for the ASBM to be viable against deployed naval targets. The ASBM must be integrated with C4ISR systems, a process that "could take years."[123] Additionally, the ASBM has yet to be tested on a sea-based mobile target. Nevertheless, the Deputy Chief of Naval Operations noted in January 2011 that China may possess "non-space based ISR [that] could provide the necessary information to support DF-21D employment."[124]

Underestimating the Speed of China's ASBM Development

U.S. monitoring of ASBM development likely increased with the 2004 publication of the PLA Second Artillery[125] book, *Science of Second Artillery Campaigns,* which described the ASBM as an "assassin's mace" against aircraft carriers.[126] The increased attention on China's ASBM program found in U.S. government papers beginning in 2009 suggests a more sustained U.S. intelligence focus on ASBM development, which correlates with concurrent reports that China's ASBM was nearing operational capability. In March 2009, DIA predicted that new Chinese ballistic missiles would become operational, though it did not specifically mention the ASBM.[127] In November 2009, Scott Bray, Senior Intelligence Officer for China at the Office of Naval Intelligence, stated that "ASBM development has progressed at a remarkable rate. In a little more than a decade, China has taken the ASBM program from the conceptual phase to nearing an operational capability."[128]

Unclassified U.S. government statements indicate that the U.S. intelligence community has been clearly aware of the development of a Chinese ASBM since at least early in the past decade.[129] According to the scholar Andrew Erickson,

---

The Quiet Surge in Space," *Project 2049: AsiaEye*, November 9, 2010. *http://blog.project2049.net/2010/11/chinas-secret-co-orbital-satellites.html.*; and Ian Easton and Mark Stokes, "China's Electronic Intelligence (ELINT) Satellite Developments: Implications for U.S. Air and Naval Operations" (Arlington, VA: Project 2049 Institute, February 23, 2011).

[123] Peh Shing Huei, "China Flexes Weapons Muscles," *Straits Times* Online, January 14, 2011. OSC Document#: SEP20110114026001.

[124] Andrew Erickson: "China Has Space Based & Non-Space-Based C2 + ISR capable of providing the targeting information necessary to employ the DF-21D Anti-Ship Ballistic Missile (ASBM*)." http://www.andrewerickson.com/2011/01/deputy-chief-of-naval-operations-for-information-dominance-n2n6-china-has-space-based-non-space-based-c2-isr-%E2%80%9Ccapable-of-providing-the-targeting-information-necessary-to-employ-the-df/.*

[125] The "Second Artillery" *(Di Er Pao Bing)* is the branch of the PLA that controls China's missile forces, in terms of both conventional missiles and China's strategic nuclear forces.

[126] Gabe Collins and Andrew Erickson, "China Deploys World's First Long-Range, Land-Based 'Carrier-Killer': DF-21D Anti-Ship Ballistic Missile (ASBM) Reaches 'Initial Operational Capability' (IOC)," *China SignPost* (洞察中国), no. 14 (December 26, 2010). For a fuller explanation of the significance of the "assassin's mace" concept, see Jason Bruzdzinski, "Demystifying Shashoujian: China's Assassin's Mace Concept," in *Civil-Military Change In China: Elites, Institutes, and Ideas After the 16th Party Congress,* eds. Andrew Scobell and Larry Wortzel (Carlisle, PA: U.S. Army War College Strategic Studies Institute, September 2004), pp. 309-364.

[127] Senate Armed Services Committee, *Statement: Annual Threat Assessment*, 111th Cong,, 1st sess., March 10, 2009. *http://www.dia.mil/public-affairs/testimonies/2009-03-10.html*.

[128] Andrew S. Erickson, "Ballistic Trajectory—China develops new anti-ship missile," *Jane's Intelligence Review* (Englewood, CO: IHS Jane's: Defense & Security Intelligence & Analysis, January 4, 2010).

[129] Senate Armed Services Committee, *Hearing to receive testimony on U.S. Pacific Command, U.S. Strategic Command, and U.S. Forces Korea in review of the Defense Authorization Request for Fiscal Year 2011 and the Future Years Defense Program*, , 111th Cong., 2nd sess., March 26, 2010; House Committee on Armed Services, *Hearing on FY 2011 National Defense Authorization Budget Requests from the U.S. Pacific Command and U.S. Forces Korea*, , 111th Cong.,2nd sess., March 25, 2010; and Richard Scott, "US believes China is poised to field ballistic anti-ship missile," *Jane's International Defence Review* (Englewood, CO: IHS Jane's: Defense & Security Intelligence & Analysis, March 2, 2010).

[The Office of Naval Intelligence] first discussed Chinese interest in ASBM development publicly in 2004; the Department of Defense in 2005. A 2006 unclassified assessment by ONI stated that "China is equipping theater ballistic missiles with maneuvering reentry vehicles (MaRVs) with radar or IR [infrared] seekers to provide the accuracy necessary to attack a ship at sea."[130]

While aware of China's ASBM development, U.S. intelligence officials have admitted to underestimating the speed at which the ASBM program has developed. In addressing the development, Vice Admiral Dorsett has said that "[w]e've been on the mark on an awful lot of our assessments but there [have also] been a handful of things we have underestimated."[131] Some commentators suggest that "open source analyses failed to foresee" the ASBM reach IOC, although it should have been apparent given broader trends in Chinese aerospace development.[132] It can be argued that many U.S. decisionmakers simply did not conceive that the centerpiece of U.S. naval supremacy, the aircraft carrier, could be challenged and held at risk. The development of the ASBM will likely encourage a rethinking of U.S. naval strategy as the ASBM becomes integrated into China's armed forces and presents a serious threat to the deployed naval forces of the United States and its allies in the western Pacific.

Factors Affecting Analysis on the Development of the Anti-Ship Ballistic Missile

Challenge #1: Increased Investment in Scientific Research & Development and Dual-Use Technologies

Over the past decade, investment in Chinese military R&D has substantially increased (see Table 2), and China currently ranks second only to the United States in overall military expenditures worldwide (to include military R&D[133]).[134] This upsurge in military expenditure over the past decade accounts in part for the increased speed observed between the development and field deployment of indigenously designed military hardware and support systems. In addition to state investments in scientific research, there is substantial private-sector investment and civilian university involvement in the research and development of new military hardware.[135] Pro-PRC media outlets have asserted that "China has the support of a complete, uninterrupted capital chain, and it has the considerable support of talented

---

[130] Andrew Erickson, "China's Anti-Ship Ballistic Missile (ASBM) Reaches Equivalent of 'Initial Operational Capability' (IOC)— Where It's Going and What It Means," February 8, 2011. *http://www.andrewerickson.com/2011/02/china%E2%80%99s-anti-ship-ballistic-missile-asbm-reaches-equivalent-of-%E2%80%9Cinitial-operational-capability%E2%80%9D-ioc%E2%80%94where-it%E2%80%99s-going-and-what-it-means/.*

[131] Karen Parrish, "Navy Intel Chief Discusses China's Military Advances," *American Forces Press Service*, January 6, 2011. *http://www.defense.gov/news/newsarticle.aspx?id=62346.*

[132] Andrew Erickson, "China's Anti-Ship Ballistic Missile (ASBM) Reaches Equivalent of 'Initial Operational Capability' (IOC)— Where It's Going and What It Means," February 8, 2011 *http://www.andrewerickson.com/2011/02/china%E2%80%99s-anti-ship-ballistic-missile-asbm-reaches-equivalent-of-%E2%80%9Cinitial-operational-capability%E2%80%9D-ioc%E2%80%94where-it%E2%80%99s-going-and-what-it-means/.*

[133] The Stockholm International Peace Research Institute's (SIPRI) definition of military expenditure should include military R&D, but due to the nontransparent nature of Chinese defense expenditure and the overlap between defense and other sectors of government, true expenditure figures are unattainable (for the full list of what is included in SIPRI's military expenditure calculations, please see *http://www.sipri.org/research/armaments/milex/resultoutput/sources_methods/definitions*).

[134] Stockholm International Peace Research Institute, *The 15 Major Spender Countries in 2009* (Table), *http://www.sipri.org/research/armaments/milex/resultoutput/milex_15.*

[135] For a detailed discussion of China's national-level science programs and state supports for scientific research, see Micah Springut, Stephen Schlaikjer, and David Chen, *China's Program for Science and Technology Modernization: Implications for American Competitiveness* (report prepared by CENTRA Technology, Inc., on behalf of the U.S.-China Economic and Security Review Commission, April 2011).

science and technology personnel; achieving high-speed development is quite normal."[136] However, the dearth of U.S. understanding of (or the underutilization in studying) Chinese open source materials and Chinese R&D practices may have contributed to U.S. underestimation of Chinese military development.

In February 2001, then President Jiang Zemin created the 998 State Security Project [also known as the "Assassin's Mace" (杀手锏 / *shashoujian*) program[137]] to "[enhance] the innovation in advanced national defense technology, stressing the development of military/civilian dual-use technology and mastering as quickly as possible the new *shashoujian* needed to safeguard our national sovereignty and security."[138] It is through dual-use programs such as the *shashoujian* program that China has successfully exploited relevant technologies for application in its defense sector.

U.S. policymakers' focus on observing and tracking the transfer of dual-use technologies to China is insufficient. Indeed, U.S.-China joint ventures and Chinese integration with the global production and R&D chain have, through the transfer of technology, know-how, and capital, "facilitated dramatic improvements in Chinese defense-industrial production and PLA modernization since the 1990s" and warrant U.S. attention.[139] Particularly relevant industries include the nuclear, missiles, shipbuilding, and defense electronics sectors. The combination of state-funded R&D programs and private industry commercial technologies has accelerated the advancement of China's military.[140]

Table 2: Official Defense Expenditure Budget, People's Republic of China, 2000–2009

YEAR	2000	2001	2002	2003	2004	2005	2006	2007	2008	2009
RMB	180	223	256	283	322	364	431	511	599	686
US$b (2008)	31.2	38.4	44.4	48.5	53.1	59	68.8	77.9	86.2	98.8
%GDP	1.8	2	2.1	2.1	2	2	2	2	2	2

RMB=renminbi (Chinese currency); GDP=gross domestic product
Source: Adapted from SIPRI Military Expenditure Database. http://milexdata.sipri.org/.

Challenge #2: Underestimating the Threat Perceptions & Political Priorities of the Chinese Leadership

The Taiwan Scenario as a Motivating Factor for PLA Modernization

China's military priority since the early- to mid-1990s has been to maintain a strategic advantage over Taiwan's military forces and—if it should ever feel compelled to initiate military operations against

---

[136] Ni Eryan, ""The Point of the Military is to Prevent Violence -- Unconfirmed Reports Convey Real Information," Hong Kong *Wen Wei Po* Online (Chinese), January 10, 2011. OSC ID: CPP20110110787012.

[137] For a fuller explanation of the "assassin's mace" concept, see Jason Bruzdzinski, "Demystifying Shashoujian: China's Assassin's Mace Concept," in *Civil-Military Change In China: Elites, Institutes, and Ideas After the 16th Party Congress,* eds. Andrew Scobell and Larry Wortzel (Carlisle, PA: U.S. Army War College Strategic Studies Institute, September 2004), pp. 309–364.

[138] Wang Congbiao, "Studying Jiang Zemin's 'On Science and Technology'," *Jiefangjun Bao*, February 13, 2001.

[139] James Mulvenon and Rebecca Samm Tyroler-Cooper, *China's Defense Industry on the Path of Reform* (Washington, DC: Defense Group Incorporated, October 2009), p. 4.

[140] Mark Stokes, *China's Evolving Conventional Strategic Strike Capability* (Arlington, VA: Project 2049 Institute, September 14, 2009), p. 21.

Taiwan—in deterring and countering any third-party (i.e., U.S.) intervention.[141] This driver for PLA force modernization was given particular impetus following the Taiwan Strait Crisis of 1996, when the PLA brass was humiliated by the dispatch of U.S. Navy aircraft carriers to the vicinity of Taiwan in reaction to PLA saber-rattling exercises, which were intended to intimidate Taiwan's populace in the midst of island-wide elections.

The 1996 Taiwan Strait crisis catalyzed investment in the long-term modernization and professionalization of China's armed forces. If there had been uncertainty before as to what the United States might do in a Taiwan scenario, this seemed to be a clear statement that U.S. forces would intervene—and that the PLA lacked effective capabilities to deter or defeat them. Even after the crisis subsided, then-CCP paramount leader Jiang Zemin was apparently convinced of the imminence of military conflict in the Strait, and reportedly advocated accelerating preparations by the PLA for taking military action against Taiwan.[142] As a result, the PLA accelerated its efforts to acquire strike assets (e.g., modern submarines, missiles, 3rd and 4th generation aircraft) that could keep American forces at bay.[143]

The anti-ship ballistic missile (ASBM) could be especially important in achieving this objective, as it is developed to target U.S. aircraft carriers. Preliminary research is believed to have begun shortly after the 1996 Taiwan Strait Crisis. Anti-satellite (ASAT) weapons are also a priority in a Taiwan contingency. Since Taiwan is thousands of nautical miles from U.S. shores, the United States would rely heavily on satellite intelligence and communications in the event of any Taiwan Strait contingency operations, and ASAT weapons could degrade and/or destroy U.S. satellite and command, control, communications, computer, intelligence, surveillance, and reconnaissance (C4ISR) capabilities. ASBMs and ASATs are just two of a wide range of anti-access/area denial (A2/AD) systems that China has been developing since the Taiwan Strait crisis.

The increase in spending is also likely fueled by the motivation to address and bridge the technological gap between the PLA and other advanced militaries in the world. While the driving motivation behind China's increased military expenditure is defending national interests on the country's periphery, China's disputed maritime claims and steadily expanding interests overseas have prompted reconsideration of China's military strategy and vision—beyond the defense of its territorial sovereignty, and into power projection and influencing the outcome of territorial claims along China's maritime periphery. In July 2009, Peter Dutton, professor of Strategic Studies at the U.S. Naval War College, pointed out the long-term nature of "Chinese research, development, and investment in military technologies designed to challenge outside access—outside naval access, in particular—to East Asian waters."[144]

The escalation in recent years of territorial and resource tensions in East Asia, geopolitical instability around China's periphery in countries such as North Korea, and an increased U.S. presence around China's declared territorial boundaries may have further prompted China to prepare to defend its maritime borders and claims in the event of military conflict, thus resulting in increased Chinese investments in military modernization and force buildup. Such increased tensions could potentially

---

[141] Office of the Secretary of Defense, *Annual Report to Congress: The Military Power of the People's Republic of China 2005* (Washington, DC: U.S. Government Printing Office, 2005), p. 7.

[142] Robert L. Suettinger, *Beyond Tiananmen: The Politics of U.S.-China Relations 1989–2000* (Washington, DC: Brookings Institution Press, 2004), p. 402; Willy Lam, "Taiwan issues keep Jiang in army role," *CNN*, November 21, 2002. *http://articles.cnn.com/2002-11-21/world/china.jiang_1_cmc-cao-gangchuan-taiwan-strait*.

[143] David Shambaugh, *Modernizing China's Military* (Los Angeles, CA: University of California Press, 2004), p. 4.

[144] Senate Committee on Foreign Relations, Subcommittee on East Asian and Pacific Affairs, *Hearing on Maritime Disputes and Sovereignty Issues in East Asia*, 111th Cong., 1st sess., July 15, 2009.

manifest themselves in conflicts with Japan (over the Senkaku/Diaoyutai Islands) or countries in the South China Sea. China might also find itself involved in military operations on the Korean Peninsula, whose stability is a source of major concern for Beijing. These geostrategic concerns have no doubt influenced China's rapid development of maritime military capabilities.

Section 4: The J-20 Fighter (Project 718)

The public unveiling of the Chengdu *Jian*-20 prototype fifth-generation stealth fighter jet on January 11, 2011 provoked an upsurge of government and media attention and speculation. According to media sources, the U.S. government was well aware of China's fifth-generation fighter but may not have fully known its state of development. An academic Chinese military publication forecasted that China would "determine final technological requirements by 2010, and will complete preparatory work for fitting out the J-20 by 2015."[145] The J-20 test flight compelled U.S. Secretary of Defense Robert Gates to reassess U.S. intelligence efforts on monitoring the speed of Chinese military development, saying China "may be somewhat further ahead in the development of the aircraft than our intelligence had earlier indicated."[146]

Significant Dates

1997	XXJ (also known as the J-XX) preliminary design phase.
1997	ONI reports that China is working on a large, multirole fighter; predicts XXJ to enter service in 2015.[147]
2003	DoD annual report projects that China's focus on fighter aircraft for the next 20 years will be F-10 and Sukhoi upgrades.[148]
2004	DoD annual report predicts that PLA Air Force will be closer to becoming a modern air force by 2010-15.[149]
2004	Taiwan Colonel (Ret.) Lo Chih-Cheng projects the J-XX (later known as the J-20) will enter service around 2010.[150]
2005	Indian Army Brigadier Govinda M. Nair predicts the introduction of the J-20 by 2015.[151]
2008	In March, Chinese media report an expected design completion by 2015.[152]
2008	Chinese officials and experts project that the J-20 will be fully operational between 2017 and 2019.[153]
2009	U.S. Secretary of Defense Robert Gates predicts that China will not have any fifth-generation aircraft before 2020.[154]

---

[145] U.S. Army Asian Studies Detachment Intelligence Information Report, "China Plans to Develop Fifth-Generation Jet Fighter," June 9, 2008. OSD ID:JPP20080610075006. The Chinese magazine referred to in the report is *Naval & Merchant Ships*, or *Jianchuan Zhishi (舰船知识)*.

[146] Wendell Minnick, "Sino-U.S. Ties Back On Track, But For How Long?" *Defense News*, January 17, 2011. *http://www.defensenews.com/story.php?i=5469851&c=FEA&s=CVS*.

[147] Richard D. Fisher Jr., "China's Fifth Generation Air Combat Ambitions: A Preliminary Assessment," September 14, 2009. http:// *www.hudson.org/files/documents/AsianAirpowerFisher.ppt.*

[148] Office of the Secretary of Defense, *Annual Report on the Military Power of the People's Republic of China 2003* (Washington, DC: U.S. Government Printing Office, 2003), p. 23.

[149] Office of the Secretary of Defense, *Annual Report on the Military Power of the People's Republic of China 2004* (Washington, DC: U.S. Government Printing Office, 2004), pp. 22–23.

[150] Lo Chih-Cheng, "The Operational Requirements for the ROCAF's Next Generation Fighters," *Taiwan Defense Affairs*, December 1, 2004. OSC ID: CPP20070209312003.

[151] Govinda M. Nair, "China's Drive to Great Power Status and the Evolution of Future Asian Security Alignments" (Carlisle, PA: U.S. Army War College, 2005), p. 11.

[152] "China's tactical and technical requirements of the final J-20 expected to be completed by 2010," [中国歼 20 最终战术技术要求预计将 2010 年完成 *Zhongguo Jian-20 Zuizhong Zhanshu Jishu Yaoqiu Yuji Jiang 2010 Nian Wancheng*], *Naval & Merchant Ships* [舰船知识 *Jianchuan Zhishi*]. *http://mil.news.sina.com.cn/p/2008-03-14/0739490073.html.*

[153] Jeremy Page, "A Chinese Stealth Challenge?" *Wall Street Journal*, January 5, 2011. *http://online.wsj.com/article/SB10001424052748703808704576061674166905408.html*.

[154] Robert Gates (speech at the Economic Club of Chicago, July 16, 2009). *http://www.defense.gov/speeches/speech.aspx?speechid=1369*.

Significant Dates, continued	
2010	U.S. officials project J-20 will enter service in 2017-2019.[155]
2011	January 11, J-20's first public test flight.
2011	April 17, J-20's second public test flight.[156]
2011	May 5, J-20's third and fourth public test flight.[157]
2011	May 12, J-20's fifth public test flight.[158]
2011	May 14, J-20's sixth public test flight.[159]
2011	August 15, J-20's twenty-seventh public test flight.[160]
2011	December (exact date unknown), J-20's sixtieth public test flight.[161]
2012	February 28, PRC media reports on continuing J-20 flight testing near Chengdu.[162]

History and Development of the J-20

In 1997, the U.S. Office of Naval Intelligence first designated the name "XXJ" to the developmental fighter now known as the J-20.[163] The Chengdu Aircraft Industry Corporation and the Shenyang Aircraft Industry Corporation, in conjunction with No. 611 and 601 Research Institutes (respectively), competed to design the prototype for this next-generation jet.[164] China reportedly has conducted preliminary research on fifth-generation technologies since the late 1990s.[165] Chinese sources state that design development began in the 1980s.[166] Chinese media reported that the J-20 completed aircraft program definition design by 2005 and was in the final state of program definition in 2008. The article acknowledged that unspecified technical problems with the fighter still existed.[167]

In 2004, the Department of Defense's annual report predicted that by 2010, China would have a "more robust fleet of fourth-generation fighters," though it made no reference to any fifth-generation fighter

---

[155] Jim Wolf, "New Chinese fighter jet expected by 2018: U.S. intelligence," Reuters, May 21, 2010. *http://www.reuters.com/article/2010/05/21/us-china-usa-fighter-idUSTRE64K0MY20100521.*

[156] *People's Daily*, "Global Times: J20 'appears' to have made second flight," April 19, 2011. *http://english.peopledaily.com.cn/90001/90776/90786/7354617.html,*

[157] "OSC Report: Photos, Video Clips Show J-20 Third, Fourth Test Flights on 5 May," May 5, 2011. OSC ID: CPP20110505658002.

[158] "PRC Website Claims J-20 Completes Fifth, Sixth Test Flights on 12, 14 May," May 17, 2011. OSC ID: FEA20110518017937.

[159] "PRC Website Claims J-20 Completes Fifth, Sixth Test Flights on 12, 14 May," May 17, 2011. OSC ID: FEA20110518017937.

[160] "China's stealth fighter J-20 conducts 27th test flight," *Xinhua*, August 15, 2011, *http://news.xinhuanet.com/english2010/photo/2011-08/17/c_131055076.htm*.

[161] People's Daily Online [人民网], "Internet Users Leak: Jian-20 Completes 60th Test Flight, Expose FC-1 Xiaolong Armed Anti-ship Missile" [网友曝：歼-20 完成第 60 次试飞 枭龙挂反舰导弹曝光 Wangyoubao: Jian-20 wancheng di 60 ci shifei, xiaolonggua fanjian daodan puguang], December 14, 2011, *http://military.people.com.cn/GB/16598038.html*.

[162] "China's J-20 Fighter Unfolds Landing Gear Bay," *People's Daily On-Line* (in English), February 28, 2012. *http://english.people.com.cn/90786/7742528.html.*

[163] *Jane's All the World's Aircraft*, "CAC J-20" (Englewood, CO: IHS Jane's: Defense & Security Intelligence & Analysis, January 28, 2011).

[164] Robert Hewison, *Teeth of the Dragon* (Englewood, CO: *Jane's Defence*, IHS Jane's: Defense & Security Intelligence & Analysis, January 19, 2011).

[165] *China's Defence Today*, "J-XX 4th Generation Fighter Aircraft., http://www.sinodefence.com/airforce/fighter/jxx.asp.*

[166] "China's tactical and technical requirements of the final J-20 expected to be completed by 2010," [中国歼 20 最终战术技术要求预计将 2010 年完成 Zhongguo Jian-20 Zuizhong Zhanshu Jishu Yaoqiu Yuji Jiang 2010 Nian Wancheng], *Naval & Merchant Ships* [舰船知识 Jianchuan Zhishi], March 14, 2008. *http://mil.news.sina.com.cn/p/2008-03-14/0739490073.html*.

[167] "Russian Specialist Unveils the Mystery of China's Fifth Generation Fighter Aircraft: The J-20," "俄专家揭秘中国第五代战机：歼-20" [E Zhuanjia Jiemi Zhongguo Diwudai Zhanji: Jian-20], *Naval & Merchant Ships* [舰船知识 Jianchuan Zhishi], March 14, 2008. *http://plaaf.net/html/53/n-23053.html*.

program.[168] In 2005, a U.S. Army War College report by Indian Army Brigadier Govinda M. Nair predicted the introduction of fifth-generation J-20s (then dubbed the XXJ) by 2015.[169] On March 14, 2008, there was a photo posted in a Xinhua forum titled "Jian-20: China Accelerates Research on Fifth-Generation Fighter Jet," although the photo was taken down soon thereafter.[170]

Figure 5: Projected Timeline of J-20 Development

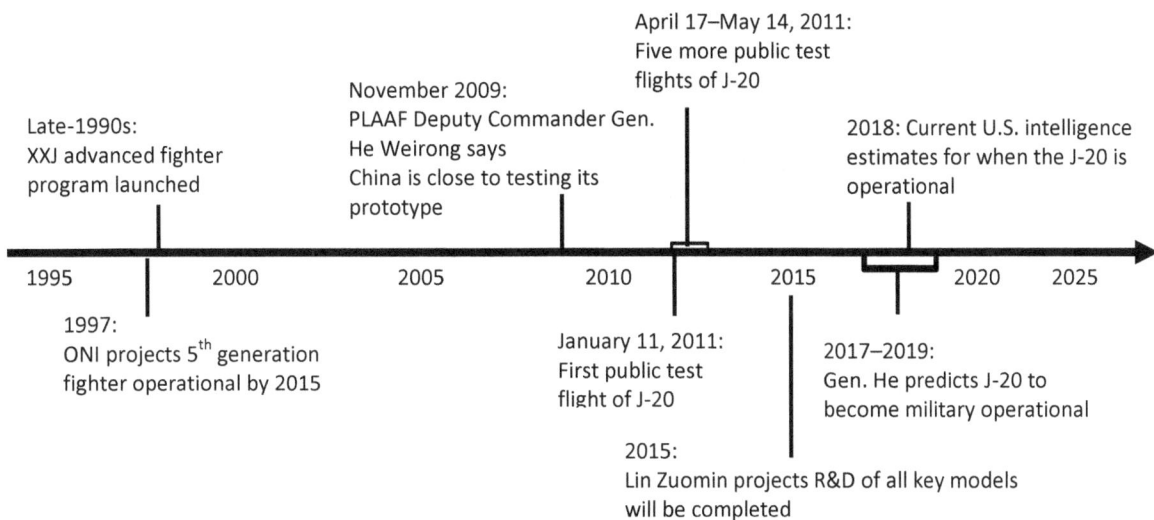

Source: Adapted from Gabe Collins and Andrew Erickson, "China's New Project 718/J-20 Fighter: Development Outlook and Strategic Implications"

In 2009, General He Weirong, deputy Air Force chief, remarked during an interview on China Central Television that a fifth-generation fighter was "currently under development" and "may soon undertake its first flight" before testing and fielding.[171] The comment was interpreted as a response to Defense Secretary Gates' comment that China would not field fifth-generation fighters until after 2020.[172] General He also projected that the new fighter would enter service between 2017 and 2019.[173] While open source analysts have for years speculated the existence of a fifth-generation fighter program, there was no official confirmation until General He's comments.[174]

---

[168] Office of the Secretary of Defense, *Annual Report on the Military Power of the People's Republic of China 2003* (Washington, DC: U.S. Government Printing Office, 2003), p. 23.

[169] Govinda M. Nair, "China's Drive to Great Power Status and the Evolution of Future Asian Security Alignments" (Carlisle, PA: U.S. Army War College, 2005), p. 11.

[170] Xinhua ,"Jian-20: China accelerates research on fifth-generation jet" [歼-20：中国加快研制第五代战机(组图) Jian-20: Zhongguo Jiakuai Yanzhi Diwudai Zhanji (Zutu)], March 14, 2008. *http://news.xinhuanet.com/forum/2008-03/14/content_7787592.htm.*

[171] Bradley Perrett, "China Close To Testing Next-Gen Fighter," *Aviation Week*, November 13, 2009. *http://www.aviationweek.com/aw/generic/story_generic.jsp?channel=awst&id=news/CHINA111309.xml.*

[172] Secretary Gates has also added that his comment meant that by 2020, there would still be a significant disparity in the number of J-20s versus U.S. fifth-generation aircraft.

[173] *People's Daily* [人民日报 Renmin Ribao], "America's Serious Intelligence Omission, China's Fourth Generation Aircraft Shakes Americans," [美惊呼对华情报严重漏报 中国大运四代机震呆老美 [Mei Jinghu Duihua Qingbao Yanzhong Loubao Zhongguo Dayun Sidaiji Zhendai Laomei], November 16, 2009. *http://military.people.com.cn/GB/8221/72028/76059/76404/10387974.html.*

[174] Bradley Perrett, "China Close To Testing Next-Gen Fighter," *Aviation Week*, November 13, 2009. *http://www.aviationweek.com/aw/generic/story_generic.jsp?channel=awst&id=news/CHINA111309.xml.* In October 2010.

There are signs that the progression toward fielding the J-20 is on track. In 2011 alone, China publicly tested the J-20 sixty times.[175]

Figure 6: Undercarriage view of a J-20 fighter in flight.

Source: *Jane's All the World's Aircraft,* "CAC J-20" (Englewood, CO: IHS Jane's: *Defense & Security Intelligence & Analysis*, January 28, 2011).

Currently, there is neither confirmation nor denial from either the U.S. or Chinese government of the exact nature and status of many of the J-20's features and performance parameters—including its reputed stealth factor—though reports of China's developing stealth material for the prototype J-XX have appeared in online Chinese forums since 2006.[176] Russian media sources have expressed doubts about its stealth capabilities, as China lacks certain key components for designing a fifth-generation fighter, such as an indigenously designed engine and on-board radar.[177] Some U.S. analysts have also voiced reservations about design challenges with the J-20—to include China's assessed difficulties with the design and production of high-performance jet engines—further adding that anti-stealth technologies are progressing rapidly and "may already be an operational capability."[178] Other doubts that have been raised focus on materials, engines, avionics and electronics, personnel, and training. The J-20s must be adequately covered with materials that diffuse heat and help reduce radar signature, and these must be maintained constantly to preserve their stealth characteristics.[179]

Factors Affecting Analysis on the Development of the J-20

---

[175] People's Daily Online [人民网], "Internet Users Leak: Jian-20 Completes 60th Test Flight, Expose FC-1 Xiaolong Armed Anti-ship Missile" [网友曝：歼-20 完成第 60 次试飞 枭龙挂反舰导弹曝光 Wangyoubao: Jian-20 wancheng di 60 ci shifei, xiaolonggua fanjian daodan puguang], December 14, 2011, *http://military.people.com.cn/GB/16598038.html*.

[176] "Highlights: PRC Military Forums 9-21 Aug 06." OSC ID: CPP20060911436001.

[177] Moscow *Argumenty Nedeli* Online, "Chinese 'Stealth'—More Invisible Than Any Other Stealth Aircraft," January 14, 2010. OSC ID: CEP20100120349010.

[178] David A. Fulghum et al., "Stealthy Chinese J-20 Vulnerable," *Aviation Week*, January 18, 2011. *http://www.aviationweek.com/aw/generic/story_generic.jsp?channel=awst&id=news/awst/2011/01/17/AW_01_17_2011_p20-281824.xml*.

[179] Gabe Collins and Andrew Erickson, "China's New Project 718/J-20 Fighter: Development Outlook and Strategic Implications," *China SignPost* (洞察中国), no. 18 (January 17, 2011*). http://www.andrewerickson.com/2011/01/j-20-fighter-development-outlook-strategic-implications/.*

Challenge #1: Underestimating the Pace of Developments in China's Aviation Sector

Despite media attention and speculation, U.S. government analysts were not surprised by the unveiling of the J-20: U.S. intelligence had reportedly been following the development of the aircraft since the mid-1990s. Nonetheless, in public statements U.S. government officials have been unclear about the time line for when the J-20 will become fully operational,[180] especially as initial estimates for prototype testing were off by a few years.[181]

Vice Admiral Dorsett has indicated that U.S. estimates on J-20 development were too conservative, saying that while the J-20 is "not a surprise....We have been pretty consistent in underestimating the delivery and IOC of Chinese technology, weapon systems. They've entered operational capability quicker [than expected]."[182] In May 2010 testimony before the Senate, Wayne Ulman, head of the U.S. National Air and Space Intelligence Center, assessed that the J-20 will be deployed around 2018.[183] Another expert, Tai Ming Cheung, predicted in early 2011 that "it will likely take another five to 10 years before the aircraft is ready for serial production."[184] Considering the increasing pace of and funding available for Chinese military modernization, U.S. officials would likely not be surprised if the J-20 enters operational capability earlier than current projections.[185]

Challenge #2: A Chinese Civil-Military Divide? Or Unclear "Strategic Communication"?

According to an unnamed senior DoD official widely cited in the media, "When Secretary Gates raised the question of the J-20 in the [January 2011] meeting with President Hu it was clear that none of the [Chinese] civilians in the room had been informed."[186] Encouraged by such comments, the first public test flight of the J-20 aircraft prompted widespread media speculation that the PLA planned the event to send a message to U.S. officials, without coordinating with the CCP civilian leadership.[187] This revived many of the questions regarding bureaucratic stovepiping, as well as conjectures about a "rogue" PLA, that had followed in the wake of the January 2007 ASAT launch.

---

[180] Vice Admiral Dorsett said in a briefing that "it's not clear when [the J-20] will be fully tested and operational." Karen Parrish, "Navy Intel Chief Discusses China's Military Advances," *American Forces Press Service*, January 6, 2011. *http://www.defense.gov/news/newsarticle.aspx?id=62346*.

[181] Sources projected the J-20 would make its maiden flight in 2012, but according to *Jane's*, "More than one anonymous Chinese source has claimed that the J-20 had been flying 'for nearly a year' by the time of its unveiling." For more information, see *Jane's All the World's Aircraft*, "CAC J-20" (Englewood, CO: IHS Jane's: Defense & Security Intelligence & Analysis, January 28, 2011).

[182] Transcript of Defense Writers Group roundtable with Vice Admiral David J. Dorsett, Deputy Chief of Naval Operations for Information Dominance, January 5, 2011.

[183] Jim Wolf, "RPT-New Chinese fighter jet expected by 2018: US Intel," Reuters, May 21, 2010. *http://www.reuters.com/article/2010/05/21/china-usa-fighter-idUSN2117451920100521*.

[184] Wendell Minnick, "Sino-U.S. Ties Back On Track, But For How Long?" *Defense News*, January 17, 2011. *http://www.defensenews.com/story.php?i=5469851&c=FEA&s=CVS.*

[185] Jeremy Page, "China Stealth Jet 'Leak' Viewed as Intentional," *Wall Street Journal*, January 8, 2011. *http://online.wsj.com/article/SB10001424052748704055204576067514151124434.html*; and Jim Wolf, "RPT-New Chinese fighter jet expected by 2018: US Intel," Reuters, May 21, 2010. *http://www.reuters.com/article/2010/05/21/china-usa-fighter-idUSN2117451920100521*.

[186] Kathrin Hille and Daniel Dombey, Stealth test flight overshadows Gates trip

[187] As one such example, see Peter Martin, "In China, Is the Gun Beginning to Command the Party?" *The Guardian* (UK), January 13, 2011. *http://www.guardian.co.uk/commentisfree/2011/jan/13/china-hu-jintao-test-flight-military*.

Given the extent to which China's leadership oversees military and technology developments, it is unlikely that President Hu was unaware of the J-20 test.[188] The strongest evidence for this is that Vice President Xi Jinping and Politburo Standing Committee member Wu Bangguo appeared at the J-20 test flight site in Chengdu on January 10, 2011, suggesting that the civilian leadership was likely aware of the J-20 testing planned for the following day.[189] While there is no clear answer to the true extent of coordination and information sharing between the civil and military leadership, "analysis of Chinese handling of the J-20 test flight raises doubts about Beijing's capacity to manage successfully its ascendance as a great power and raises a question as to whether a civil-military 'gap' exists in China's peaceful rise."[190]

If the test flight was intended as a form of strategic communication, the message may have been deterrent in nature: i.e., that China is developing advanced weapons of its own, and should not be taken lightly by foreign military forces.[191] However, this is speculative, and it is unknown whether the J-20 flight represented strategic communication at all, or if it was simply a routine event that happened to coincide with a major diplomatic visit. This case provides another example of the challenges posed to outside observers by the Chinese military's lack of transparency, and by the opaque nature of the government's decision-making processes.

Beijing's selective transparency regarding J-20 developments has led to widespread speculation regarding the future development and implications of the aircraft.[192] Dr. Erickson argues that the publicized testing "resemble[d] a muted strategic communication" to display the progress of China's military modernization.[193] To assuage U.S. concerns about the rapid pace of China's military modernization, the Pentagon has communicated the message that the J-20's capabilities should not be overhyped or overstated. Pentagon spokesman Geoff Morrell has emphasized that the United States does not know the true extent of J-20 development and has urged "everybody to...slow down a little bit on our characterizations of the J-20 at this point."[194] Nevertheless, the dissemination of information on the development status of the J-20 has prompted the United States to reassess its military strategy and force posture in the Western Pacific in order to maintain military superiority over potential adversaries.[195]

Conclusions

[188] Richard D. Fisher, Jr., "Stealthy Progress: Spotlight Falls on China's Airpower Ambitions," *Jane's Intelligence Review* (Englewood, CO: IHS Jane's: Defense & Security Intelligence & Analysis, February 1, 2011).

[189] Gabe Collins and Andrew Erickson, "China's New Project 718/J-20 Fighter: Development Outlook and Strategic Implications," *China SignPost* (洞察中国), 18 (January 17, 2011). *http://www.andrewerickson.com/2011/01/j-20-fighter-development-outlook-strategic-implications/*.

[190] U.S.-China Economic and Security Review Commission, *Hearing on China's Narratives Regarding National Security Policy*, testimony of Mark Stokes; U.S.-China Economic and Security Review Commission, *Hearing on China's Narratives Regarding National Security Policy*, written testimony of Andrew Scobell, March 10, 2011; and Andrew Scobell, "Is There a Civil-Military Gap in China's Peaceful Rise?" *Parameters* 39:2 (Summer 2009): 4–22.

[191] U.S.-China Economic and Security Review Commission, *Hearing on China's Narratives Regarding National Security Policy*, written testimony of Andrew Scobell, March 10, 2011.

[192] Gabe Collins and Andrew Erickson, "China's New Project 718/J-20 Fighter: Development Outlook and Strategic Implications," *China SignPost* (洞察中国), no. 18 (January 17, 2011). *http://www.andrewerickson.com/2011/01/j-20-fighter-development-outlook-strategic-implications/*.

[193] Gabe Collins and Andrew Erickson, "China's New Project 718/J-20 Fighter: Development Outlook and Strategic Implications," *China SignPost* (洞察中国), no. 18 (January 17, 2011). *http://www.andrewerickson.com/2011/01/j-20-fighter-development-outlook-strategic-implications/.*

[194] U.S. Department of Defense: Office of the Assistant Secretary of Defense (Public Affairs,) "DOD News Briefing with Geoff Morrell from the Pentagon," January 26, 2011. *http://www.defense.gov/transcripts/transcript.aspx?transcriptid=4758*.

[195] *Chosun Ilbo*, "Chinese Weapons Advances Prompt US Rethink of Stance Toward China's Capability,"January 13, 2011.

Based on open source research on the four cases covered in this report, there are no universal trends in the success of U.S. government estimates on the development of indigenous Chinese weapons. Particular considerations for each of these case studies are:

- The available evidence suggests that the United States did not expect the development of the *Yuan*-class submarines—much less that the Chinese Navy had potentially acquired and installed AIP systems in its newer submarines.
- Although the United States was keenly aware of Chinese ASAT development, exact details of the January 2007 test may have been unexpected. Additionally, the seeming lack of coordination among PRC government agencies in regards to the launch highlighted gaps in U.S. understanding of the PRC's decision-making processes for national security issues.
- The United States apparently underestimated the speed of development of the anti-ship ballistic missile, which reportedly reached IOC in December 2010.
- The United States also may have underestimated the speed of development of China's fifth-generation fighter jet, the J-20, although the true extent of the aircraft's capabilities remain unclear.

An immediate concern for the United States involves China's upcoming leadership transition in 2012. The United States must understand the political leanings of China's fifth-generation leaders and consider any potential changes in military and political policy. For example, one expert on PRC leadership politics has stated that Xi Jinping "is a keen supporter of funneling more national resources toward military modernization."[196] Understanding the processes of Chinese civilian and military leadership decision-making, and the rhetoric they use in both internal policy debates and official explanations of finished policy to domestic and foreign audiences, is essential to avoid future lapses in the anticipation and understanding of Chinese military developments. As China continues to expand economically, politically, technologically, and militarily, if the United States and other allied powers fail to forecast—or at least anticipate—these developments, the future balance of power in the Asia-Pacific region may be significantly impacted.

There is a clear trend that China is modernizing its military forces both to defend its borders and to assert its growing presence in the region.[197] Nevertheless, it is important to consider several factors that may influence U.S. analysis on Chinese indigenous military and technical developments:

- China's selective transparency strategy may inhibit U.S. decisionmakers' understanding of the true state of China's military development, as well as its strategic intentions. To address this concern, the United States has made it a priority to monitor Chinese military development,[198] but gaps in understanding remain.
- Potentially poor policy coordination between the PRC's civilian and military leadership may also complicate efforts to analyze China's national security policy decision-making processes and the course of PRC military modernization.

---

[196] Willy Lam, "The Military Maneuvers of Xi Jinping," *Wall Street Journal*, January 26, 2011.

[197] *Xinhua News Service* (in English), "China Will Achieve Modernization of Military and Defense: DM"), December 29, 2010. http://english.cri.cn/6909/2010/12/29/2742s612494.htm.

[198] Joint Chiefs of Staff, *The National Military Strategy of the United States of America 2011*. http://www.jcs.mil/content/files/2011-02/020811084800_2011_NMS_-_08_FEB_2011.pdf.

- Increased military expenditures catalyzed by hypothetical Taiwan scenarios, conflicting territorial claims, and geopolitical competition in the Asia-Pacific region contribute to the speed of procurement, development – and, ultimately, field deployment – of more advanced indigenous Chinese weapons systems.
- Understanding the variety of R&D methods, as well as watching for trends in the development of dual-use technologies, will assist U.S. analysts to better gauge Chinese progress in technology and/or weapons development.
- The current dearth of cleared U.S. analysts with the ability to read Chinese,[199] as well as the commitment of U.S. resources to its engagements in the Middle East, diverts attention and resources away from a larger focus on China analysis.[200]

As the updated 2011 National Military Strategy (among other public statements by U.S. officials) indicates, U.S. analysts closely monitor Chinese developments.[201] According to other public statements by U.S. officials such as Defense Secretary Gates, there is also a larger focus on developing programs that counter Chinese (and other potential adversaries') technological advances intended to target U.S. weaknesses.[202] Lieutenant General Wallace Gregson (USMC, ret.), former Assistant Secretary of Defense for Asian and Pacific Security Affairs, has advocated developing capabilities such as modern integrated air defense systems to deter and defeat China's emerging asymmetric capabilities in cyber warfare, anti-satellite warfare, and anti-ship weaponry.[203]

The development of the most prominent indigenously designed weapons systems unveiled by the PLA over the past decade caught many private analysts off guard, but did not surprise the U.S. government. However, government analysts have underestimated the speed at which these systems developed and reached initial operating capability. There is a clear trend in increased U.S. government focus on tracking Chinese military developments, and analysts now appear to be more aware that contemporary Chinese technological developments are proceeding at a considerably faster rate than the timelines observed in Soviet or PRC historical norms.

---

[199] Central Intelligence Agency, "CIA Director Calls for a National Commitment to Language Proficiency at Foreign Language Summit, Press Release, December 8, 2010. *https://www.cia.gov/news-information/press-releases-statements/press-release-2010/foreign-language-summit.html*.

[200] For argumentation that a focus on terrorism and Middle Eastern issues has distracted the U.S. intelligence community from longer-term analysis on other regions of the world, see Roger Z. George, "Reflections on CIA Analysis: Is It Finished?" *Intelligence and National Security*, 26:1 (2011).

[201] *The National Military Strategy of the United States of America 2011* explicitly and frequently mentions China. *http://www.jcs.mil/content/files/2011-02/020811084800_2011_NMS_-_08_FEB_2011.pdf*.

[202] Secretary Gates is quoted as saying: "Well, we obviously have to be mindful...of the Chinese military modernization programs, their anti-ship cruise and ballistic missiles that potentially can put our aircraft carriers at risk, new fifth-generation aircraft.... So they have a lot of capabilities that they're building. But we need to be mindful of that. We need to be in a position to deal with those capabilities in the future." Robert Gates (Secretary of Defense), television interview with Jim Lehrer, "Gates on Pentagon Cuts, Implementing DADT, China's Military Build-up," *PBS* NewsHour, January 6, 2011. *http://www.pbs.org/newshour/bb/military/jan-june11/gates2_01-06.html.*

[203] Senate Committee on Armed Services, *Hearing on Nominations Before the Senate Armed Services Committee* , 111th Cong., 1st sess., April 28, 2009.

Appendix: Controversies Regarding Competing Analysis on Chinese Military Developments

The apparent disparity over the past decade between U.S. predictions and the actual pace of development in Chinese indigenous weapons systems raises questions as to whether flawed underlying assumptions may have affected analysis in this area, inside or outside the U.S. government. This continues a controversy of long standing: for over a decade U.S. intelligence and policymaking circles have seen a vigorous debate regarding both the pace of PLA modernization, as well as the PRC's intentions regarding the future use of its armed forces.

In one prominent and controversial example, the U.S. House of Representatives Permanent Select Committee on Intelligence attached comments to the intelligence appropriations bill for the year 2000 that expressed concerns about the quality of analysis on China emerging from the CIA. Specifically, the committee asserted the need

> to subject the China-Taiwan Issues Group in the Central Intelligence Agency's Directorate of Intelligence to rigorous external competitive analysis to ensure that this key analytical component is held to the highest analytic standards possible. The committee has directed the Deputy Director for Intelligence to expose CIA's China analysts to "contrary thinking" to challenge their suppositions and analytical methodologies more aggressively, and to forestall any possibility of "group think." [204]

As one element of this mandated "rigorous external competitive analysis," a commission was created under the leadership of Gen. John Tilelli (U.S. Army, ret.), a former commander of U.S. Forces Korea, to evaluate the quality of CIA analysis on China. The commission's July 2001 report was not made public, but reportedly criticized the CIA for unduly minimizing the potential military threat from China.[205] For their part, unnamed intelligence officials were quoted in the press as criticizing the external reviews on the grounds that they were intimidating to agency personnel, and risked politicizing the intelligence process.[206]

Similarly, controversial external analysis regarding China's military development was seen in the 2008 report "China's Strategic Modernization," produced by the State Department's International Security Advisory Board (ISAB). The ISAB report presented a more pessimistic picture than the official views expressed by the State Department itself: Stating, for example, that "[T]he United States is viewed as China's principal strategic adversary," and that "Chinese military modernization is proceeding at a rate to be of concern even with the most benign interpretation of China's motivation."[207]

---

[204] "Report Together With Additional Views [To Accompany H.R. 1555]—Intelligence Authorization Act For Fiscal Year 2000," U.S. House of Representatives Permanent Select Committee on Intelligence (106th Cong., 1st Sess.), May 7, 1999. *http://www.loyola.edu/departments/academics/political-science/strategic-intelligence/intel/hrpt106-130.pdf*.

[205] William Safire, "The CIA's China Tilt," *New York Times*, July 9, 2001.

[206] Richard J. Newman and Kevin Whitelaw, "China: How Big a Threat?" *U.S. News & World Report*, July 23, 2001.

[207] "China's Strategic Modernization: Report from the ISAB Task Force," Department of State International Security Advisory Board, October 2008. *http://www.fas.org/nuke/guide/china/ISAB2008.pdf*.

Assumptions Affecting Analysis on China

The underlying assumptions held by analysts are fundamental: Analysts with contrasting assumptions regarding the nature and goals of the Chinese government can examine the same evidence and reach diametrically opposed conclusions.[208] A list of commonly-held assumptions in the late 1990s regarding PLA modernization might have included:

1. That China's defense industry would continue to be a low priority for development relative to other economic sectors;
2. That the Chinese defense industry would continue the patterns of slow progress (or lack thereof) observable in the 1980s and early 1990s;
3. That China's defense industry would remain highly dependent on purchases of advanced foreign military technology, without the capacity to effectively engineer (or reverse-engineer) similar equipment;
4. That the PRC maintains a very defensive, inward-looking defense posture, which would not require the development of weapons systems intended for air and naval power projection;
5. That Chinese military personnel would be incapable of measuring up to U.S. standards; and/or
6. That all of these considerations are largely moot to begin with, as the government of the PRC has a benign role in the international arena and will neither threaten its neighbors or pose a challenge to U.S. interests.[209]

One example of such thinking may be seen in a 2001 article from _U.S. News and World Report,_ which stated that

> _China, with a decrepit industrial base and a risk-averse socialist bureaucracy, faces even more difficulty than advanced nations in developing high-tech weaponry... [and] Beijing's Communist leadership appears far more concerned about threats from inside China than about extending its military reach... China also faces a mounting financial crunch... [and furthermore] Chinese troops appear to be minor leaguers compared with their American counterparts. Many U.S. experts blamed the April [2001] collision between an EP-3 surveillance plane and a Chinese fighter jet on poor skills by the Chinese pilot.[210]_

While particular points within these assumptions have held up over time—for example, China's aviation industry continues to face difficulties in producing modern aircraft engines[211]—the perspective of a decade has revealed many of them to be seriously flawed. The most prominent mistaken assumptions have been:

---

[208] For a detailed exploration of this issue as it relates to U.S.-China policy, see Josh Kerbel, "Thinking Straight: Cognitive Bias in the US Debate about China," _Studies in Intelligence_, vol. 48 no. 3, 2004.

[209] As an illustration of the latter point, author James Mann has noted a strong trend of opinion within U.S. academic, business, and policymaking circles to emphasize the benign nature of the Chinese government, the commonality of U.S.-China interests, and the progress of democratic reform in China—a body of thought that he terms the "soothing scenario." See James Mann, _The China Fantasy: How Our Leaders Explain Away Chinese Repression_ (New York, NY: Viking Penguin, 2007), pp. 1-7.

[210] Richard J. Newman and Kevin Whitelaw, "China: How Big a Threat?" _U.S. News & World Report_, July 23, 2001.

[211] Gabe Collins and Andrew Erickson, "Jet Engine Development in China: Indigenous High-Performance Turbofans Are a Final Step Toward Fully Independent Fighter Production," _China SignPost_ (洞察中国), No. 39 (26 June 2011). _http://www.chinasignpost.com/2011/06/jet-engine-development-in-china-indigenous-high-performance-turbofans-are-a-final-step-toward-fully-independent-fighter-production/._

- *That China's "risk-averse socialist bureaucracy" could not adapt itself to the production of more modern weapons systems:* Mainstream analysis failed to anticipate the adaptability of China's state-owned armaments corporations. It also failed to foresee the extent to which China's entry into world markets, and the attendant exposure of Chinese industries to international best practices in management and manufacturing, helped to support a "dramatic and successful transformation [of China's defense industry] surpassing the expectations of even the most forward-leaning analyst."[212]
- *That PLA personnel would be incapable of matching the levels of tactical proficiency and military professionalism displayed by U.S. servicemembers:* While levels of training and professional development in the PLA continue to lag behind U.S. forces—particularly in the senior enlisted ranks—the PLA has made impressive strides over the past decade in raising standards of training, personnel compensation, and doctrinal development.[213] It is logically unfounded—and arguably expressive of a complacent sense of cultural superiority—to assume that PLA personnel are incapable of achieving higher standards of military professionalism relative to U.S. forces.
- *That the Chinese government will maintain a constrained foreign policy and an entirely defensive, inward-looking military posture:* The conventional wisdom failed to appreciate the sense of threat that China's leaders feel regarding the capabilities and intentions of the "hegemonic" United States, and the impetus this provides to China's military modernization.[214] Similarly, it also failed to predict the far more assertive behavior displayed by the PRC in pursuing its territorial claims in 2010-2011, and the seriousness of the PRC's longer-term intent to displace U.S. influence and presence in Asia.

Reconsidering Assumptions on China

There are a number of reasons that these assumptions were formed, and why they may have been resistant to change. For one, the PRC defense industry saw little substantive advancement in the 1980s and early 1990s. Continued lack of progress and reform was the most obvious assumption to make; and in many, if not most cases, predictions of continuity in past observable phenomena will prove to be accurate. However, paradigm shifts can and do occur, catching even experts by surprise. As noted by longtime Defense Intelligence Agency analyst Cynthia Grabo,

> *there is an inherent great reluctance on the part of many individuals and probably most bureaucratic organizations to stick their necks out on problems which are new, controversial, and above all which could be bad news for higher officials and the policymaker. The effect of these factors and possibly others, individually and collectively, can be to retard the analysis and acceptance of data in the intelligence system by weeks, months and sometimes even years.[215]*

---

[212] James Mulvenon and Rebecca Samm Tyroler-Cooper, *China's Defense Industry on the Path of Reform* (report prepared on behalf of the U.S.-China Economic and Security Review Commission) (Washington, DC: Defense Group Inc., October 2009), p. 4. *http://www.uscc.gov/researchpapers/2009/DGIReportonPRCDefenseIndustry--FinalVersion_10Nov2009.pdf*.

[213] Frederic Vellucci Jr., Collins Alt, Larry Ferguson II, Daniel M. Hartnett and Kenneth Allen, *The Science of PLA Training: Analysis and Overview of PLA Training Theory* (Alexandria, VA: CNA, 2009).

[214] For a discussion of views of the United States held by China's leaders, see Yong Deng, "Hegemon on the Offensive: Chinese Perspectives on U.S. Global Strategy," *Political Science Quarterly* 116: 3 (2001); and Michael Chase, "Chinese Suspicions and US Intentions," *Survival*, Volume 53 Issue 3, June 2011; and

John Lee, "China's America Obsession," *ForeignPolicy.com*, May 6, 2011. *http://www.foreignpolicy.com/articles/2011/05/06/china_s_america_obsession?page=0,0*.

[215] Cynthia Grabo, *Anticipating Surprise: Analysis for Strategic Warning* (Washington, DC: Joint Military Intelligence College Center for Strategic Intelligence Research, December 2002), p. 45.

Secondly, the conventional wisdom *zeitgeist* of the late 1990s held that liberalized trade with China would help to bring about democratic reform in China, as well as more positive relations with the United States. As President Clinton wrote in January 2000, "[World Trade Organization membership will strengthen the forces of reform inside China and thereby improve the odds that China will continue and even accelerate its gradual progress toward joining the rules-based community of nations."[216] Similarly, future Secretary of State Condoleezza Rice stated in 1999 that "Economic liberalization [in China] is ultimately going to lead to political liberalization—that's an iron law... [the Communist Party is] living on borrowed time."[217]

In fairness, many of China's observable trend lines in the 1990s appeared to point in the direction of continued economic reform, with the hope of attendant political reform. However, the course of Chinese economic reform significantly reversed course in the 2000s, turning back in the direction of increased state control over the economy.[218] The democratic reforms predicted at the turn of the century have not occurred, and under the leadership of CCP General Secretary Hu Jintao since 2002 the Chinese government has cracked down even harder on dissent and further tightened controls on the media.[219]

Paradigms of thinking about China that were formed in the late 1990s have proven very resistant to change. Experts in human cognition have noted the strong reluctance of the human mind to reconsider views once they are formed, and the strong tendency for

> *data received incrementally [to be] fit easily into an analyst's previous image. This perceptual bias is reinforced by organizational pressures favoring consistent interpretation; once the analyst is committed in writing, both the analyst and the organization have a vested interest in maintaining the original assessment.[220]*

This tendency can be reinforced even further in "expert" analysis: those who have devoted many years of study to an issue tend to have firmly formed views, and are more resistant to reconsidering their opinions in light of new evidence than are newcomers to the subject.[221] However, despite such psychological and institutional reluctance to reconsider previously held views, the pattern of the past decade indicates that the U.S. China-watching community writ large—in government, business, media, academia, and the think tank community—should reconsider much of the past conventional wisdom regarding the future course of China's rise in general, and its military modernization in specific.

---

[216] President William Clinton, "Letter to Congressional Leaders on Permanent Normal Trade Relations with China," January 24, 2000; contained within *Public Papers of the Presidents of the United States, Administration of William J. Clinton, 2000-2001, Book 1, January 1 to June 26, 2000* (Washington, DC: Office of the Federal Register, National Archives and Records Administration Staff, 2001), pp. 113-115.

[217] Condoleezza Rice, as quoted in Jay Nordlinger, "Star-in-Waiting: Meet George W.'s Foreign-Policy Czarina," *National Review*, August 30, 1999. *http://old.nationalreview.com/flashback/nordlinger200411170605.asp*.

[218] Derek Scissors, "Deng Undone: The Costs of Halting Market Reform in China," *Foreign Affairs*, May/June 2009.

[219] As two references among dozens that could be cited, see Benjamin Joffe-Walt, "China's Leaders Launch Smokeless War Against Internet and Media Dissent, *The Guardian* (UK), September 26, 2005; and Willy Lam, "Hu's Crackdown on Political Dissent," *China Brief*, Vol. 5 Issue 13, June 7, 2005. *http://www.jamestown.org/single/?no_cache=1&tx_ttnews[tt_news]=3866*.

[220] Richards J. Heuer, *The Psychology of Intelligence Analysis* (Langley, VA: Central Intelligence Agency Center for the Study of Intelligence, 1999), p. 16.

[221] This topic is dealt with in depth in Philip E. Tetlock, *Expert Political Judgment: How Good Is It? How Can We Know?* (Princeton, NJ: Princeton University Press, 2005).

A decade on, it is now clear that much of the conventional wisdom about China dating from the turn of the century has proven to be dramatically wrong. These predictive errors carry with them serious geopolitical consequences. To avoid being similarly caught off-guard in 2022, U.S. analysts should carefully reexamine many of their widely-held assumptions about the Chinese government and its policy goals.